THE
CAULIFLOWER
COOKBOOK

HEATHER THOMAS

THE
CAULIFLOWER
COOKBOOK

HEATHER THOMAS

EBURY
PRESS

CONTENTS

MAIN MEALS

SIDES & PRESERVES

BAKING

INTRODUCTION

Cauliflower used to be perceived as rather humble and understated but it's now one of the most popular vegetables around with surging sales and the celebrity status of a culinary star. No longer just served as a modest side dish or as cauliflower cheese, it's become a staple for many meat eaters as well as vegetarians and vegans. As more of us are graduating towards plant-based, low-carb and gluten-free diets, cauliflower is a popular choice and an essential part of the trend towards eating more mindfully.

WHAT MAKES CAULIFLOWER SO SPECIAL?

The keys to cauliflower's success are its versatility and flexibility. Its mild, nutty and slightly sweet taste makes it ideal for absorbing the flavours of other foods, ranging from powerful chillies and pungent herbs to more subtle and gentler spices. It also lends itself to many diverse cooking methods: it can be boiled or steamed; mashed or puréed; deep-fried or stir-fried; baked or roasted; stewed or casseroled; or even pickled or just served raw.

We have inspirational recipes for everything from a whole roasted cauliflower served as a centrepiece to crisp golden cauliflower 'buffalo wings'. Cauliflower steaks are spiced, roasted and served like their meaty counterparts. The florets are pulverised into rice-like grains in a food processor and used in salads, risotto, 'rice' dishes, pizza crust and even in cakes, muffins and cookies.

HISTORY & VARIETIES

Cauliflower has been cultivated and eaten in Cyprus for over 2,000 years. It moved from there to Turkey, the Levant and Egypt, Italy, Spain and northwest Europe. It is also now very popular in China and India. Most varieties have a dense white round head (the 'curd') composed of individual florets, surrounded by green leaves. However, there are also some more colourful varieties, such as the distinctive green Italian Romanesco, which is pointed and more conical, as well as brown, orange, purple and yellow variations.

NUTRITION & HEALTH BENEFITS

Like other members of the Brassica family, cauliflower packs quite a nutritional punch. It's rich in vitamins C, K, B6, folate and pantothenic acid as well as dietary fibre and a jackpot of minerals, including iron, manganese, magnesium, potassium and phosphorus. Full of phyto-nutrients, especially antioxidants, it's the tenth best source of vitamin C. One serving of cauliflower can provide 73 per cent of our recommended daily vitamin C intake.

And with practically zero grams of fat and carbs, it's the slimmer's friend – a great aid to weight loss as well as for maintaining a healthy weight. As a carb substitute for white rice or flour it is impressive with only 25kcals and 5g carbs per 100g compared to 150kcals and 34g carbs for regular rice. It also has triple the fibre content of rice. No wonder it is becoming so popular as a flour substitute in pizza bases, cakes, muffins, brownies and cookies.

It's the healthy choice for people who want to eat a gluten-free diet, and it's nearly free of fat, sugar and sodium. What's not to like? Eating cauliflower regularly can reduce our risk of developing cancer, especially prostate cancer, and it's good for heart health, helping to protect the lining of our arteries. Because it's rich in antioxidants with a neuroprotective capacity as well as choline, which is essential for maintaining and repairing the brain, it enhances working memory and reduces the risk of developing dementia, Alzheimer's and Parkinson's disease.

ABOUT THE RECIPES

This book celebrates cauliflower in all its varieties and chameleon-like adaptability – as a traditional comfort food as well as an original substitute in many carb and meat-based dishes. Most of the recipes will appeal to vegetarians although a few do contain meat or fish. And there's lots of choice for vegans, too.

We have collected recipes from all over the world to make the book truly international as well as including some of the most innovative and trending ways of preparing, cooking and serving cauliflower. There's everything from using fried cauliflower slices as 'sliders' for burgers or bases for bruschetta and *cicchetti* to cauliflower risotto, pizza bases, jerked 'steaks', roasted 'chips' and even breakfast muffins and squidgy chocolate brownies. There really is something for everyone, regardless of cooking skills or expertise.

PREPARATION & COOKING

Cauliflower is really easy to prepare and cook. You can blitz the white florets (curds) in a food processor to make 'rice'; slice them through the stem in thick 'steaks' for roasting in the oven; grate them to make tabbouleh; simmer, steam, boil or fry them; coat them in white sauce for a classic cauliflower cheese and purée them for savoury patties and fritters.

HOW TO PREPARE & COOK CAULIFLOWER RICE:

Cut the cauliflower into quarters and remove and discard the stalk and leaves. Separate the white curd into small florets and blitz them in a food processor until you have very small pieces with the consistency of rice grains. If you don't have a food processor, use a medium-holed box grater to grate the florets into 'rice'.

You can use the 'rice' raw in salads, fry it in 1 tablespoon olive or vegetable oil for about 5 minutes until tender, or add it to stir-fries. Alternatively cook the raw cauliflower rice in the microwave: place it in a glass bowl, cover with clingfilm (plastic wrap) and microwave on high for 3 minutes.

HOW TO PREPARE & COOK CAULIFLOWER STEAKS:

Trim the base of the stalk, including any leaves, and discard. Cut down through the stalk, slicing the cauliflower into four 2.5cm/1in thick 'steaks'. Brush both sides with olive oil or vegetable oil and flavour with ground spices, crushed chilli flakes, herbs, curry paste, sea salt flakes, black pepper, etc. Place on a baking (cookie) sheet lined with foil or baking parchment and roast in a hot oven until cooked through, golden brown and starting to char.

TIP: When you're preparing a cauliflower don't throw away the green leaves, their stems and the thick base. They are full of flavour and nutritional goodness and can be added to other vegetable trimmings for making a delicious stock.

SNACKS & STARTERS

CHEESY ROASTED CAULIFLOWER 'CHIPS'

SERVES: 4-6 | **PREP:** 10 MINUTES | **COOK:** 20-25 MINUTES

1 medium cauliflower
3 tbsp olive oil
a pinch of crushed dried
    chilli flakes
sea salt flakes, for sprinkling
115g/4oz (1 cup) grated
    Parmesan cheese
finely chopped flat-leaf
    parsley or chives,
    for sprinkling

We've all heard of potato, sweet potato, carrot and beetroot (beet) chips but did you know that you can also make them with cauliflower? They're healthy, delicious and so easy to prepare and cook.

1 Preheat the oven to 200°C, 400°F, gas mark 6. Line a large baking (cookie) sheet with baking parchment.

2 Trim the stem away from the cauliflower and cut the head into quarters. Cut out the central stem to separate the florets. Cut the florets into 5mm/¼in thick slices.

3 Arrange the cauliflower slices, in a single layer, on the lined tray. Drizzle them with oil and sprinkle with the chilli and salt flakes.

4 Bake for 15–20 minutes until they are starting to brown and are just tender but still retain their 'bite'.

5 Sprinkle the grated Parmesan over the top and pop back in the oven for 5 minutes, or until crisp and golden brown.

6 Sprinkle with the chopped herbs and leave to cool. Serve warm or cold.

OR YOU CAN TRY THIS...
– Before roasting, sprinkle the cauliflower with a pinch of garlic powder or Italian seasoning.
– Use grated Cheddar, Grana Padano or Pecorino instead of Parmesan.
– For a special occasion, drizzle with truffle oil instead of olive oil.

CAULIFLOWER BRUSCHETTA

MAKES: 8 | **PREP:** 15 MINUTES | **COOK:** 20 MINUTES

2 tbsp extra virgin olive oil,
  plus extra for oiling and
  brushing
1 small cauliflower,
  trimmed, stem removed
  and separated into florets
1 onion, thinly sliced
2 garlic cloves, crushed
1 tsp sugar
50g/2oz (½ cup) pine nuts
50g/2oz (scant ½ cup)
  sultanas (golden raisins)
2 tsp balsamic vinegar
a squeeze of lemon juice
a few sprigs of flat-leaf
  parsley, finely chopped
8 slices ciabatta
sea salt and freshly ground
  black pepper

Most of us associate bruschetta with chopped tomatoes but this Sicilian-style *agrodolce* (sweet and sour) cauliflower and onion topping is a delicious and unusual alternative.

1 Preheat the oven to 200°C, 400°F, gas mark 6. Lightly oil a baking (cookie) sheet.

2 Cut the cauliflower florets into slices and arrange them in a single layer on the oiled baking sheet. Brush with olive oil and bake for 15 minutes.

3 Meanwhile, heat the 2 tablespoons of oil in a frying pan (skillet) over a medium heat and cook the onion and garlic, stirring occasionally, for 8–10 minutes until softened and golden. Stir in the sugar, pine nuts, sultanas, balsamic vinegar and lemon juice. Season to taste with salt and pepper.

4 Coarsely smash the roasted cauliflower and add to the onion mixture with the parsley.

5 Preheat the grill (broiler) to high. Brush the ciabatta slices with olive oil and grill (broil) on both sides until they are toasted and crisp around the edges. Pile the cauliflower mixture on top and serve immediately.

OR YOU CAN TRY THIS...
– Add some grated Parmesan or crumbled feta cheese.
– Use red wine vinegar and orange juice instead of balsamic and lemon juice.
– Mix the smashed cauliflower with chopped tomatoes and spring onions (scallions).

CAULIFLOWER CICCHETTI

SERVES: 6 | **PREP:** 15 MINUTES | **COOK:** 20 MINUTES

3 tbsp olive oil, plus extra
   for brushing
2 small cauliflowers, stems
   trimmed, cut into
   1cm/½in slices
2 garlic cloves, crushed
a pinch of crushed dried red
   (bell) pepper flakes or
   crushed dried chilli flakes
50g/2oz (½ cup) grated
   Parmesan cheese
sea salt and freshly ground
   black pepper

For the tomato topping:
400g/14oz ripe tomatoes,
   deseeded and chopped
1 garlic clove, crushed
3 tbsp fruity olive oil
a few basil leaves, torn

Cicchetti are the Venetian equivalent of Spanish tapas. They are traditionally served as snacks with an *ombra* (a glass of wine) or a *spritz* in the picturesque backstreet wine bars (*bacari*). They include a wide range of ingredients, from meatballs and raw fish to bread, toast and grilled polenta topped with liver, cured meat and seafood *in saor* (in sweetened vinegar).

1 Preheat the oven to 200°C, 400°F, gas mark 6. Lightly brush a large baking (cookie) sheet with oil.

2 Arrange the cauliflower slices on the baking sheet in a single layer. Mix the olive oil, garlic and red pepper or chilli flakes together and drizzle over the cauliflower. Season lightly with salt and pepper.

3 Bake the cauliflower for 20 minutes, turning halfway, until it is crisp and golden brown around the edges and just tender (it should retain some 'bite').

4 Meanwhile, make the tomato topping: mix all the ingredients together in a bowl and season to taste with salt and pepper.

5 Sprinkle the hot cauliflower slices with Parmesan and then top with the tomato mixture. Serve immediately while the cauliflower is still warm.

OR YOU CAN TRY THIS...
– Top with sliced, griddled cherry or baby plum tomatoes or chopped roasted vegetables.
– Try stir-fried spinach with garlic and lemon as an alternative topping.
– Add a dusting of paprika or cayenne to the cauliflower steaks.

CRISPY ANDALUSIAN CAULIFLOWER TAPAS

SERVES: 6 | **PREP:** 10 MINUTES | **COOK:** 15 MINUTES

1 small cauliflower, trimmed, stem removed and separated into florets
4 tbsp plain (all-purpose) flour
1 tsp smoked paprika
light olive oil, for deep-frying
1 tbsp red wine vinegar or lemon juice
2 tbsp capers
1 garlic clove, crushed (optional)
a few sprigs of flat-leaf parsley, finely chopped
sea salt and freshly ground black pepper
lemon wedges, to serve

These crisp golden brown cauliflower florets are sometimes served as a tapas plate in southern Spain. They are delicious eaten hot with a glass of chilled sherry. The Spanish use nutty-tasting gram (chickpea) flour for dusting the florets. If you have some, try it!

1 Steam the cauliflower florets or cook them in a pan of boiling salted water for about 5 minutes, or until they are just tender but still retain a little bite. Drain immediately.

2 Transfer to a bowl and add the flour and smoked paprika and some seasoning. Gently turn the florets until they are evenly coated all over.

3 Heat the oil in a deep pan or wok or a deep-fryer, if you have one. When it reaches 190°C, 375°F (you can use a sugar thermometer to check) add some of the florets and fry until golden brown and crisp (about 5 minutes). Remove with a slotted spoon and drain on kitchen paper (paper towels). Fry the remaining florets, in batches, in the same way.

4 Drizzle with vinegar or lemon juice, and sprinkle with sea salt, capers, garlic (if using) and parsley. Serve hot with some lemon wedges for squeezing.

OR YOU CAN TRY THIS...
– Add some heat by substituting chilli powder for the smoked paprika.
– For a milder flavour, use sweet paprika.
– Serve with tartare sauce or some mayo mixed with chopped herbs and capers.

CAULIFLOWER 'BUFFALO WING' TORTILLAS

SERVES: 4 | **PREP:** 20 MINUTES | **COOK:** 25 MINUTES

1 medium cauliflower,
   trimmed, stem removed
   and separated into florets
1 tbsp olive oil plus extra
   for oiling
2 tsp garlic granules
2–3 tbsp hot sauce,
   e.g. Sriracha
2 tbsp light mayonnaise
   or vegan mayo
5 tbsp Greek yoghurt
   or dairy-free yoghurt
   alternative
a small handful of chives
   or coriander (cilantro),
   chopped
4 large corn or wholewheat
   tortillas
2 large carrots, grated
75g/3oz rocket (arugula)
1 ripe avocado, peeled,
   stoned (pitted) and
   thinly sliced
sea salt and freshly ground
   black pepper

Roasted spicy 'buffalo wing' style cauliflower florets are served in tortillas with salad and a herby yoghurt dressing. Alternatively, for a lower calorie option, wrap everything up in large iceberg lettuce leaves instead of tortillas.

1 Preheat the oven to 220°C, 425°F, gas mark 7.

2 Cut the cauliflower florets into bite-sized pieces and toss with the olive oil and garlic granules to coat them lightly. Season with salt and pepper and spread them out on a baking (cookie) sheet.

3 Bake in the oven for 15 minutes, then brush with the hot sauce and cook for a further 10 minutes, or until crisp and golden brown on the outside and tender inside.

4 Mix together the mayonnaise and yoghurt in a bowl and stir in the chopped herbs. Season to taste.

5 Warm the tortillas in the oven or in an oiled griddle (grill) pan. Divide the grated carrot and rocket between them and top with the avocado and cauliflower. Drizzle the yoghurt dressing over the top and roll up the tortillas. Eat immediately.

OR YOU CAN TRY THIS...

– Use ready-made ranch dressing instead of the yoghurt one above.
– Add a little lemon juice and grated lemon zest to the dressing.
– Add sliced tomato or cucumber.
– Substitute guacamole for the avocado.
– Serve the cauliflower 'buffalo wings' as a snack with a tasty dip, such as fresh hot tomato salsa or some tzatziki.

CAULIFLOWER RICE SUSHI

SERVES: 4 | **PREP:** 30 MINUTES | **COOK:** 2-3 MINUTES | **CHILL:** 15 MINUTES

1 medium cauliflower, trimmed, stem removed and separated into florets
2 tbsp rice vinegar
1 tsp mirin
4 nori sheets
115g/4oz thinly sliced smoked salmon, cut into long strips
1 tsp wasabi paste
¼ cucumber, peeled, deseeded and cut into long strips
1 avocado, peeled, stoned (pitted) and cut into long strips
1 tbsp black sesame seeds
sea salt
pickled ginger and Japanese soy sauce, to serve

Try making this delicious carb-free sushi at home – it's much easier than it looks. You can buy the Japanese ingredients (wasabi paste, mirin, pickled ginger and nori sheets) in most supermarkets and delis.

1 Put the cauliflower florets in a food processor and pulse until you have rice-sized 'grains'.

2 Steam or cook the 'rice' in the microwave on high, for 2–3 minutes (see page 11). Stir in the rice vinegar and mirin, add salt to taste, and press gently with kitchen paper (paper towels) to absorb any excess liquid.

3 Place the nori sheets, shiny side down, on a bamboo sushi mat or a worktop covered with clingfilm (plastic wrap). Divide the cauliflower rice between the sheets, spreading it out evenly and level and pressing down with the back of a spoon. Leave a 1cm/½in border along the long edges.

4 Place the smoked salmon on top of the 'rice' and dot with wasabi paste. Top with the cucumber and avocado and sprinkle with sesame seeds. Using the clingfilm and sushi mat (if using) to help you, lift the long bottom edge of each nori sheet over the filling and carefully roll up towards the top, pressing down firmly as you go. When you get to the top, brush lightly with a little water to seal it.

5 Put the rolls in the fridge and leave for at least 15 minutes. Just before serving, cut them into 2.5cm/1in thick slices and serve with pickled ginger and some soy sauce for sprinkling or dipping.

OR YOU CAN TRY THIS...
– Add some hot sauce or mayonnaise to the sushi.
– Use raw sushi-grade salmon instead of smoked.
– Substitute canned tuna, cooked crab meat, peeled cooked prawns (shrimp) or even tuna mayo for the salmon.
– For a vegetarian version, omit the salmon and add some thin asparagus.

CAULIFLOWER RAREBIT

SERVES: 4 (SNACK) OR 2 (LIGHT MEAL) | **PREP:** 15 MINUTES | **COOK:** 10-12 MINUTES

1 small cauliflower, trimmed, stem removed and separated into florets
115g/4oz (½ cup) mascarpone cheese
1 tsp mustard with honey
115g/4oz (1 cup) grated Parmesan cheese
4 slices wholegrain or multi-seed bread
a good pinch of cayenne pepper
a few sprigs of flat-leaf parsley or chives, snipped
sea salt and freshly ground black pepper

This variation on cauliflower cheese on toast is both filling and satisfying; you could serve it with a crisp salad for a light lunch or supper, in which case allow 2 toasts per portion.

1 Cut the florets into small bite-sized pieces and steam or cook them in a pan of boiling salted water for about 5 minutes, or until they are just tender but still retain a little bite. Drain well.

2 Mix the mascarpone, mustard and Parmesan in a bowl. Season with salt and pepper and gently stir in the cooked cauliflower.

3 Preheat the grill (broiler) to high and lightly toast the bread on both sides. Spoon the cheesy cauliflower mixture over the toasted slices and dust with cayenne.

4 Cook the topped toasts under the hot grill, for 3–4 minutes until really hot, bubbling and golden brown. Serve immediately, sprinkled with parsley or chives.

OR YOU CAN TRY THIS...
– Use Dijon or English mustard.
– Use light soft cheese instead of mascarpone to reduce the calories and fat content.
– Experiment with different cheeses, e.g. Caerphilly, Cheddar, Emmental or Gruyère.
– Add some chopped ham, bacon or prosciutto to the cauliflower and cheese mixture.

CAVOLFIORI FRITTI

SERVES: 4-6 | **PREP:** 10 MINUTES | **COOK:** 15-20 MINUTES

1 small cauliflower,
   trimmed, stem removed
   and separated into florets
2 medium free-range eggs,
   beaten
115g/4oz (generous 1 cup)
   dried breadcrumbs
   e.g. panko
3 tbsp light olive oil
15g/½oz (1 tbsp) unsalted
   butter
115g/4oz (1 cup) grated
   Grana Padano cheese
sea salt and freshly ground
   black pepper

Pan-fried cauliflower is a popular family dish all over Italy and makes a great appetiser. For the best results it's important not to overcook the cauliflower when steaming or boiling it before coating and frying it.

1 Steam the cauliflower florets or cook them in a pan of boiling salted water for about 5 minutes, or until they are just tender but still retain a little bite. Do not overcook them. Plunge into cold water and drain immediately. Pat dry with kitchen paper (paper towels).

2 Pour the beaten eggs into a shallow bowl and put the breadcrumbs on a large plate. Season with a little salt and pepper.

3 Dip the cauliflower florets in the egg, gently shaking off any excess, and then into the breadcrumbs to coat them thinly.

4 Heat the oil and butter in a large frying pan (skillet) set over a medium to high heat. When it's hot, fry a few cauliflower florets at a time, turning them once or twice until they are crisp and golden brown all over (about 5 minutes). Remove with a slotted spoon and drain on kitchen paper. Fry the remaining florets, in batches, in the same way.

5 Sprinkle the hot cauliflower with grated cheese and serve immediately.

OR YOU CAN TRY THIS...
– Omit the butter and just use oil.
– Try a different cheese, such as Parmesan or Pecorino.
– Season the beaten eggs with a pinch of dried herbs, garlic salt or Italian seasoning.
– Add some finely chopped fresh parsley or crushed garlic to the breadcrumbs.

CAULIFLOWER CHEESE CROQUETTES

SERVES: 4-6 | **PREP:** 25 MINUTES | **CHILL:** 2 HOURS | **COOK:** 15 MINUTES

1 tbsp olive oil, plus extra
   for greasing
1 medium cauliflower,
   trimmed, stem removed
   and separated into florets
50g/2oz (¼ cup) butter
75g/3oz (¾ cup) plain
   (all-purpose) flour,
   plus extra for dusting
500ml/17fl oz (generous
   2 cups) skimmed milk
1 tsp Dijon mustard
115g/4oz (1 cup) grated
   Cheddar cheese
2 medium free-range eggs,
   beaten
115g/4oz (generous 1 cup)
   dried breadcrumbs
   e.g. panko
vegetable oil, for
   deep-frying
sea salt and freshly ground
   black pepper
lemon wedges, to serve

Crisp and golden, these yummy croquettes are great as a snack, party canapé, served with pre-dinner drinks or as an appetiser. You can prepare them in advance and chill in the fridge before frying or baking them just before serving.

1 Preheat the oven to 200°C, 400°F, gas mark 6. Lightly oil a baking (cookie) sheet.

2 Cut the cauliflower florets into bite-sized pieces and arrange in a single layer on the oiled baking sheet. Drizzle with 1 tablespoon olive oil and bake for 15 minutes.

3 Meanwhile, make the white sauce: melt the butter in a large pan set over a medium heat. Stir in the flour to make a roux (paste) and cook for 2–3 minutes. Start whisking in the milk, a little at a time, until it's all added and you have a smooth sauce. Turn up the heat and cook, stirring all the time, until it's thick and glossy.

4 Off the heat, stir in the mustard and grated cheese and season to taste. Gently stir in the cauliflower florets and transfer to a bowl. Leave to cool, then cover with clingfilm (plastic wrap) and chill in the fridge for at least 2 hours.

5 Just before cooking, pour the beaten eggs into a shallow bowl and put the breadcrumbs on a large plate. With lightly floured hands, take spoonfuls of the cauliflower mixture and mould them into small cylinders. Dip them into the beaten egg and then coat with the breadcrumbs.

6 Heat the oil in a deep pan or wok or deep-fryer, if you have one. When it reaches 190°C, 375°F (you can use a sugar thermometer to check) add a few croquettes and fry for about 3 minutes until golden brown and crisp. Remove with a slotted spoon and drain on kitchen paper (paper towels). Fry the remaining croquettes, in batches, in the same way.

7 Serve the croquettes, piping hot, sprinkled with sea salt, with some lemon wedges for squeezing.

OR YOU CAN TRY THIS...
– Add some chopped herbs to the cheesy cauliflower mixture.
– Mix 2 tablespoons finely grated Parmesan with the breadcrumbs.
– Add a good pinch of cayenne pepper to the breadcrumbs.
– Serve with tzatziki or chilled yoghurt drizzled with hot sauce or swirled with harissa.

TIP: For a healthier version, bake the croquettes for 20–25 minutes on an oiled baking sheet in a preheated oven at 200°C, 400°F, gas mark 6 until crisp and golden.

CAULIFLOWER, POTATO & SPINACH SAMOSAS

SERVES: 8 | **PREP:** 30 MINUTES | **COOK:** 35-40 MINUTES

450g/1lb potatoes, peeled
    and cubed
1 small cauliflower,
    trimmed, stem removed
    and separated into florets
1 tbsp sunflower oil, plus
    extra for brushing
1 large onion, finely
    chopped
2 garlic cloves, crushed
1 red chilli, diced
1 tsp grated fresh root
    ginger
2 tsp black mustard seeds
1 tbsp mild curry paste
225g/8oz baby spinach
a handful of coriander
    (cilantro), chopped
8 sheets filo (phyllo) pastry
sea salt and freshly ground
    black pepper
chilled yoghurt and mango
    chutney, to serve

Spicy vegetable samosas are so delicious and much easier to make than you might think. Baking them in the oven is healthier than frying them and they taste just as good.

1 Preheat the oven to 200°C, 400°F, gas mark 6. Line a baking (cookie) sheet with baking parchment.

2 Cook the cubed potatoes in a pan of boiling salted water or a steamer for 10–12 minutes until just tender – they should not be soft and mushy. Drain well.

3 Cut the cauliflower florets into small bite-sized pieces and steam or cook in boiling salted water for about 5 minutes, or until they are just tender but still retain a little bite. Drain well.

4 Meanwhile, heat the oil in a large pan set over a low heat and cook the onion and garlic, stirring occasionally, for 6–8 minutes until softened. Add the chilli, ginger and mustard seeds and cook for 2 minutes. Stir in the curry paste and cook for 1 minute.

5 Add the spinach and 2 tablespoons water, cover the pan and cook for 2 minutes until the leaves wilt. Gently stir in the coriander, cooked potatoes and cauliflower. Season with salt and pepper, then set aside to cool.

6 Place one sheet of filo pastry on a clean worktop and brush lightly with oil. Cover with another sheet and brush with oil. Cut lengthways down the middle into 2 long rectangles. Place a large spoonful of the cooled filling on the top right-hand corner of each strip of pastry. Fold the pastry over the filling at an angle to make a triangle, then keep on folding it over until you get to the bottom of each strip and have a neat triangular parcel. Repeat with the remaining sheets of filo pastry and the filling mixture to make 8 samosas.

7 Brush the samosas lightly with oil and place on the lined baking sheet. Bake for 20–25 minutes until crisp and golden. Serve hot or warm with a bowl of chilled yoghurt and mango chutney.

OR YOU CAN TRY THIS...
– Use frozen peas instead of spinach.
– Add some cumin seeds and a pinch of ground turmeric.
– A cooling cucumber raita makes a good accompaniment.

LIGHT MEALS
& SALADS

CAULIFLOWER RICE & CHICKEN SALAD

SERVES: 4 | **PREP:** 20 MINUTES | **COOK:** 6-8 MINUTES | **CHILL:** 15 MINUTES

1 small cauliflower, trimmed, stem removed and separated into florets

2 tbsp groundnut (peanut) oil

2 lemongrass stalks, peeled and diced

1 red chilli, diced

1 bunch of spring onions (scallions), thinly sliced

75g/3oz (generous 1 cup) grated carrot

75g/3oz (generous 1 cup) grated courgette (zucchini)

3 cooked chicken breast fillets, skinned and shredded

3 fresh kaffir lime leaves, shredded

1 bunch of mint, finely chopped

1 bunch of coriander (cilantro), finely chopped

For the citrus dressing:
juice of 2 limes

2 tbsp nam pla (Thai fish sauce)

1 tbsp caster (superfine) sugar

This colourful salad is so easy to make and full of citrus, spicy, salty and sweet flavours. And because it's so healthy and carb-free you don't have to worry about how much you eat. You can make it in advance and keep it for several hours or even overnight in the fridge.

1 Put the cauliflower florets in a food processor and pulse until they have the consistency of rice-sized 'grains'.

2 Heat the oil in a wok or deep frying pan (skillet) over a medium to high heat. Add the lemongrass, chilli and spring onions and stir-fry for 2–3 minutes. Add the cauliflower rice and stir-fry for 4–5 minutes until warm and tender but still slightly crunchy.

3 Transfer the 'rice' to a large bowl and stir in the grated vegetables, chicken, lime leaves and herbs.

4 Blend all the dressing ingredients together until well mixed. Sprinkle over the salad and toss gently.

5 Cover the bowl with a lid or some clingfilm (plastic wrap) and chill in the refrigerator for at least 15 minutes, or until required.

OR YOU CAN TRY THIS...

– Use cooked prawns (shrimp) instead of chicken.

– Vary the chopped herbs – try sweet Thai basil or regular basil leaves.

– If you don't have groundnut oil, use sunflower or light olive oil.

CAULIFLOWER TABBOULEH SALAD

SERVES: 4 | **PREP:** 20 MINUTES | **COOK:** 15-30 MINUTES

1 large cauliflower, trimmed, stem removed and separated into florets
juice of 2 lemons
6 tbsp fruity olive oil
1 garlic clove, crushed
1 red onion, finely chopped
350g/12oz cherry tomatoes, chopped
1 large bunch of flat-leaf parsley, finely chopped
a handful of mint, finely chopped
a pinch of crushed dried red (bell) pepper flakes or crushed dried chilli flakes
sea salt and freshly ground black pepper

If you're trying to eat less carbs and go gluten-free, using grated cauliflower instead of bulgur wheat in a tabbouleh is a healthy and delicious alternative. If you're in a hurry, you can pulse the cauliflower florets in a food processor until they resemble grains of rice.

1 Using the largest holes of a box grater, coarsely grate the cauliflower florets into little 'crumbs'.

2 Transfer to a large bowl and stir in the lemon juice, olive oil and garlic. Season lightly with salt and pepper and set aside for at least 15–30 minutes.

3 Add the red onion, tomatoes, herbs and red pepper or chilli flakes. Stir well to combine. Check the seasoning and serve.

OR YOU CAN TRY THIS...

– Vary the herbs: try coriander (cilantro) and basil.
– Stir in some baby spinach or rocket (arugula), diced red (bell) pepper or cucumber just before serving.
– Drizzle with pomegranate molasses.
– Add some pine nuts or chopped pistachios for extra crunch.

TIP: You can make this salad up to 3 days in advance if you keep it in a sealed container in the fridge. The flavours develop with time.

CAULIFLOWER RICE PILAF

SERVES: 4 | **PREP:** 15 MINUTES | **COOK:** 8-10 MINUTES

1 large cauliflower, trimmed, stem removed and separated into florets
2 tbsp sunflower, rapeseed or light olive oil
1 bunch of spring onions (scallions), thinly sliced
2 garlic cloves, crushed
a good pinch of ground cinnamon
1 tsp ground cumin
a pinch of crushed dried chilli flakes
75g/3oz (½ cup) sultanas (golden raisins)
grated zest and juice of 1 small lemon
a handful of flat-leaf parsley, chopped
50g/2oz (½ cup) chopped toasted pistachios
seeds of ½ pomegranate or pomegranate molasses, for drizzling
sea salt and freshly ground black pepper

This delicious pilaf is a healthy low-carb alternative to the real dish, which is made with rice. Crunchy, colourful and subtly spiced, it's great served with a salad or some roasted vegetables. Pop any leftovers into a sealed container and chill in the fridge overnight to eat the following day as a packed lunch.

1 Put the cauliflower florets in a food processor and pulse until they have the consistency of rice-sized 'grains'.

2 Heat the oil in a large frying pan (skillet) set over a medium to high heat. Add the spring onions and garlic and cook for 2–3 minutes until starting to colour. Stir in the ground spices and chilli flakes and cook for 1 minute.

3 Reduce the heat and add the sultanas and cauliflower rice and cook, stirring occasionally, for 3–4 minutes, or until the cauliflower is hot and starting to soften a little (it should still retain some crunch). Stir in the lemon zest and juice and parsley. Season to taste with salt and pepper.

4 Transfer the pilaf to a serving bowl and sprinkle with the pistachios and pomegranate seeds or drizzle with pomegranate molasses. Serve warm.

OR YOU CAN TRY THIS...
– Use shallots or red onion instead of spring onions.
– Walnuts, hazelnuts, pine nuts or almonds work well.
– Experiment with different spices: allspice, ground coriander and ground turmeric.
– Use cumin seeds instead of ground cumin.
– Stir some rocket (arugula) or baby spinach into the warm pilaf.

CAULIFLOWER BURGERS WITH FENNEL SALAD

SERVES: 4 | **PREP:** 20 MINUTES | **CHILL:** 15-30 MINUTES | **COOK:** 20 MINUTES

1 medium cauliflower, trimmed, stem removed and separated into florets
2 tbsp olive oil, plus extra for shallow frying
1 onion, chopped
2 garlic cloves, crushed
1 tsp ground cumin
a pinch of chilli powder
400g/14oz can chickpeas, rinsed and drained
a handful of flat-leaf parsley or mint, chopped
1 tbsp plain (all-purpose) flour, plus extra for dusting
grated zest and juice of 1 small lemon
sea salt and freshly ground black pepper

Cauliflower is such a versatile vegetable. Did you know that it makes delicious burgers? Here they are served with a crisp, crunchy, zingy fennel salad. If your burger mixture is too wet, just add some more flour. If it's falling apart and the burgers don't hold their shape, bind it with some beaten egg.

1 Cook the cauliflower florets in a pan of boiling salted water for 10–12 minutes until just tender, not mushy. Drain well.

2 Meanwhile, heat the oil in a frying pan (skillet) over a medium heat and cook the onion and garlic for 6–8 minutes until softened and golden. Stir in the spices and season with salt and pepper.

3 Put the cauliflower and chickpeas in a bowl and mash coarsely with a potato masher. The mixture should not be smooth so don't worry about the lumpy texture. Stir in the cooked onion and garlic, herbs, flour and lemon zest together with enough lemon juice to bind the mixture together. Set aside to cool.

4 When the mixture is really cool, divide it into 4 equal portions and shape each one into a burger. Dust with flour and chill in the fridge for 15–30 minutes to firm up.

For the fennel salad:
1 large fennel bulb
2 sweet juicy oranges
1 ripe avocado, peeled, stoned (pitted) and cubed
a handful of black olives, stoned (pitted)
sea salt crystals, for sprinkling
fruity green olive oil, for drizzling
warm pitta breads, cut into triangles, to serve

5 For the salad: thinly slice the fennel, reserving the green feathery fronds. Cut all the peel and pith off the oranges and slice horizontally into rounds. Mix in a large bowl with the avocado and olives. Chop the reserved fennel leaves and sprinkle over the salad with the salt crystals. Drizzle with olive oil.

6 Heat a little olive oil – not too much, just 1–2 tablespoons – in a large frying pan over a medium to high heat. Cook the burgers for 2–3 minutes on each side until golden brown. Drain on kitchen paper (paper towels).

7 Serve the burgers with the fennel salad and warm pitta breads.

OR YOU CAN TRY THIS...

– Use canned butter (lima) beans or cannellini beans instead of chickpeas.
– Serve the burgers in buns topped with tzatziki or yoghurt swirled with harissa.
– Use a diced chilli instead of chilli powder.

SPICY CHICKPEA & CAULIFLOWER BUDDHA BOWL

SERVES: 4 | **PREP:** 15 MINUTES | **COOK:** 25-30 MINUTES

1 medium cauliflower, trimmed, stem removed and separated into florets
1 red onion, cut into wedges
5 tbsp olive oil
2 x 400g/14oz cans chickpeas, rinsed and drained
½ tsp fine sea salt
1 tsp chilli powder
1 tsp ground cumin
1 tsp smoked paprika
75g/3oz (generous ¼ cup) stoned (pitted) dates, cut into thin slivers
seeds of 1 pomegranate
a handful of flat-leaf parsley, finely chopped
sea salt and freshly ground black pepper

For the yoghurt and tahini dressing:
250g/9 oz (1 cup) Greek yoghurt
2 tbsp tahini
1 garlic clove, crushed
2 tbsp olive oil
grated zest and juice of 1 lemon

This crunchy salad is surprisingly filling and full of aromatic spicy flavours. It's really healthy and nutritious, too – perfect for a light lunch or supper.

1 Preheat the oven to 200°C, 400°F, gas mark 6.

2 Toss the cauliflower florets and red onion wedges in 3 tablespoons of the olive oil and spread them out in a single layer on a baking (cookie) sheet. Season lightly with salt and pepper.

3 Put the chickpeas in a bowl with the remaining olive oil, the fine sea salt and spices and stir until they are evenly coated. Spread them out in a single layer on a second baking sheet.

4 Roast both trays of vegetables for 25–30 minutes, turning the cauliflower, red onion and chickpeas once or twice until they are crisp and golden brown. The cauliflower should be tender but retain a little crunch.

5 Meanwhile, put all the dressing ingredients in a large bowl and mix together well, season to taste with salt and pepper.

6 Divide the roasted cauliflower, onion, chickpeas, dates, pomegranate seeds and dressing between your serving bowls. Sprinkle with the chopped parsley and serve warm or at room temperature.

OR YOU CAN TRY THIS...
– To make this salad more substantial, add roasted carrots, squash, sweet potatoes, aubergine (eggplant) or (bell) peppers.
– Use chopped coriander (cilantro) or mint instead of parsley.
– Add some bitter salad leaves (radicchio, chicory and rocket, for example) and baby plum tomatoes to the bowls.

WARM AEGEAN CAULIFLOWER SALAD

SERVES: 4 | **PREP:** 15 MINUTES | **COOK:** 5-7 MINUTES

1 medium cauliflower,
   trimmed, stem removed
   and separated into florets
a handful of dill, chopped
a handful of juicy olives,
   stoned (pitted)
1 bunch of spring onions
   (scallions), thinly sliced
115g/4oz feta cheese,
   crumbled (optional)
sea salt and freshly ground
   black pepper

*For the oil and lemon
   dressing:*
120ml/4fl oz (½ cup)
   fruity green olive oil
juice of 1 large lemon
1 garlic clove, crushed

On many Aegean islands, in the intense heat of a Greek summer, lots of salads are served lukewarm and simply dressed with olive oil and lemon juice. Unusual though it sounds, it's a very appetising way to serve many cooked vegetables that are more flavourful eaten warm than chilled.

1 Whisk all the dressing ingredients together in a bowl. Set aside while you cook the cauliflower.

2 Steam the cauliflower florets or cook in a pan of boiling salted water, for 5–7 minutes until just tender but still slightly crisp. Drain well and pat dry with kitchen paper (paper towels).

3 Transfer the cauliflower to a large bowl and add the dill, olives and spring onions. Grind a little sea salt and black pepper over the top and toss gently in the dressing.

4 Serve warm with some feta cheese crumbled over the top (if using).

OR YOU CAN TRY THIS...

– Mix in some chopped ripe tomatoes and diced cucumber.
– Use a diced red onion instead of spring onions for a sharper taste.
– Add some dried *rigani* (Greek oregano) to the dressing.
– Instead of steaming or boiling the cauliflower, roast it with olive oil.

CAULIFLOWER CHEESE SOUP

SERVES: 4 | **PREP:** 15 MINUTES | **COOK:** 45 MINUTES

25g/1oz (2 tbsp) butter
1 tbsp olive oil
1 onion, chopped
2 celery sticks, chopped
2 garlic cloves, crushed
1 large potato, peeled and diced
1 medium cauliflower, trimmed and cut into chunks
1 litre/1¾ pints (4 cups) hot vegetable stock
1 bay leaf
200ml/7fl oz (scant 1 cup) half fat crème fraîche
2 tsp wholegrain mustard
115g/4oz (1 cup) grated mature Cheddar cheese, plus extra to garnish
a few chives, snipped
cayenne pepper, for dusting
sea salt and freshly ground black pepper
crusty bread, to serve

This comforting homely soup is perfect on chilly winter evenings when you feel like eating something simple and warming. Make sure you use a large potato as it helps to thicken the soup.

1 Heat the butter and oil in a large pan set over a low to medium heat. Cook the onion, celery and garlic, stirring occasionally, for 6–8 minutes until tender but not browned. Stir in the potato and cauliflower and cook for 1 minute.

2 Add the hot stock and the bay leaf to the pan and simmer gently for 25–30 minutes until the vegetables are tender. Remove the bay leaf.

3 Blitz the soup, in batches, in a food processor or blender until smooth. Return to the pan and stir in the crème fraîche, mustard and Cheddar. Stir gently over a low heat until the cheese melts into the creamy soup. Season to taste with salt and pepper.

4 Ladle the soup into bowls and sprinkle with extra grated cheese and chives. Dust with cayenne pepper and serve immediately with crusty bread.

OR YOU CAN TRY THIS...
– For a milder flavour use Gruyère cheese.
– Garnish with croûtons or crumbled crisply grilled (broiled) bacon.
– Add some diced carrot or parsnip to the soup.

CAULIFLOWER TACOS WITH GUACAMOLE

SERVES: 4 | **PREP:** 25 MINUTES | **COOK:** 20-25 MINUTES

2 tbsp light olive or
  sunflower oil, plus extra
  for oiling
1 medium cauliflower,
  trimmed, stem removed
  and separated into florets
1 tsp garlic powder
2–3 tbsp buffalo hot sauce
¼ red or white cabbage,
  finely shredded
8 regular tortillas
a handful of coriander
  (cilantro), chopped

For the guacamole sauce:
½ red onion, diced
1 green chilli, diced
1 garlic clove, crushed
½ tsp sea salt crystals
2 ripe avocados, peeled and
  stoned (pitted)
juice of 2 limes
1 small bunch of coriander
  (cilantro), chopped
1 ripe tomato, deseeded
  and diced
4 tbsp plain yoghurt

Tacos are a healthy option when you fill them with red-hot cauliflower buffalo wings and homemade guacamole sauce.

1 Preheat the oven to 230°C, 450°F, gas mark 8. Oil a large baking (cookie) sheet.

2 Toss the cauliflower florets in the 2 tablespoons of oil and garlic powder and spread them out, in a single layer, on the oiled sheet. Bake for 15 minutes until golden brown. Coat them with the hot sauce and return to the oven for 5–10 minutes until really crisp.

3 Meanwhile, make the guacamole sauce: crush the red onion, chilli, garlic and salt crystals in a pestle and mortar. Mash the avocado flesh with a fork and add the lime juice, coriander and tomato and the red onion mixture. Mix well and then stir in the yoghurt.

4 Toss the cabbage in some of the guacamole sauce, reserving the rest. Warm the tortillas in the hot oven.

5 Divide the shredded cabbage and cauliflower between the tortillas. Sprinkle with coriander and drizzle with the remaining guacamole sauce. Enjoy!

OR YOU CAN TRY THIS...

– Instead of cabbage, try shredded carrots, sliced celery, spring onions (scallions), cucumber or mangetout (snow peas).
– Use ready-made guacamole and thin it with lime juice and yoghurt.

MINI CAULIFLOWER 'PIZZAS'

SERVES: 4 | **PREP:** 20 MINUTES | **COOK:** 25-30 MINUTES

For the cauliflower pizza base:
1 large cauliflower,
    trimmed, stem removed
    and separated into florets
115g/4oz (¾ cup) ground
    almonds (almond meal)
3 tbsp grated Parmesan
    cheese
1 garlic clove, crushed
1 tbsp olive oil
2 medium free-range eggs,
    beaten
sea salt and freshly ground
    black pepper

No more worrying about the calories now that you can eat carb and gluten-free pizza! The delicious base is made with healthy cauliflower and ground almonds, and it's so easy to prepare and cook.

1 Preheat the oven to 200°C, 400°F, gas mark 6. Line 2 large baking (cookie) sheets with baking parchment.

2 Put the cauliflower florets in a food processor and pulse until they have the consistency of 'crumbs'. Transfer to a glass bowl, cover with clingfilm (plastic wrap) and microwave on high for 3–4 minutes. Spoon the cauliflower on to a stack of kitchen paper (paper towels) or a clean tea towel and press out any liquid until the grains are dry.

3 Mix the cauliflower in a large bowl with the ground almonds, Parmesan, garlic, olive oil, beaten eggs and a little salt and pepper until the mixture forms a dough-like ball. Alternatively, blitz everything together in a food processor until smooth.

4 Divide the mixture into 2 portions and shape each one into a ball. Place on the lined baking sheets and flatten and stretch them out with your hands to form 1cm/½in thick circles. Cook in the oven for 15 minutes, or until cooked through and golden. Remove the pizzas and increase the oven temperature to 230°C, 450°F, gas mark 8.

For the topping:
1 tsp olive oil
400g/14oz can chopped
  tomatoes
1 tsp sugar
1 tbsp tomato purée (paste)
a splash of balsamic vinegar
100g/3¾oz mozzarella,
  thinly sliced
12 black olives, stoned
a few basil leaves
green pesto, for drizzling

5 Meanwhile, heat the oil in a frying pan (skillet) over a medium to high heat. Add the tomatoes, sugar and tomato purée and cook for 6–8 minutes until thick and reduced. Add the balsamic and season with salt and pepper, to taste.

6 Spread the tomato mixture over the pizza bases and top with the mozzarella and olives. Bake in the oven for 5–10 minutes, or until the cheese is bubbling.

7 Serve cut into wedges, sprinkled with fresh basil and drizzled with pesto.

OR YOU CAN TRY THIS...
– Add some roasted vegetables to the topping: chunks of squash, aubergine (eggplant), red onion or red and yellow (bell) peppers.
– Top the cooked pizzas with rocket (arugula) and some wafer-thin Parma ham.

TERIYAKI CAULIFLOWER WITH SESAME NOODLES

SERVES: 4 | **PREP:** 15 MINUTES | **COOK:** 25-30 MINUTES

1 medium cauliflower, trimmed, stem removed and separated into florets

1–2 tbsp sunflower or rapeseed (canola) oil

250g/9oz medium egg noodles

2 tbsp toasted sesame oil

350g/12oz mushrooms, sliced

1 bunch of spring onions (scallions), sliced

2.5cm/1in piece fresh root ginger, peeled and finely diced

1 tbsp toasted sesame seeds

For the teriyaki sauce:
2 tbsp dark soy sauce

1 tbsp mirin

1 tbsp sake

1 tbsp clear honey

2 garlic cloves, crushed

Even though you have to pre-roast the cauliflower, this stir-fry makes a quick and easy light meal. Don't worry if you haven't got all the ingredients for the teriyaki sauce – just use the bottled ready-made sort instead.

1 Preheat the oven to 190°C, 375°F, gas mark 5.

2 Put the cauliflower florets and sunflower or rapeseed oil in a bowl and toss until the florets are lightly coated. Arrange them in a single layer on a baking (cookie) sheet and roast in the oven for 20 minutes, or until tender and starting to brown.

3 Meanwhile, cook the egg noodles following the pack instructions. Drain.

4 Mix all the teriyaki sauce ingredients together in a bowl.

5 When the cauliflower is cooked, heat the sesame oil in a large wok or deep frying pan (skillet) over a high heat. Stir-fry the mushrooms, spring onions and ginger for 3–4 minutes until tender. Tip in the teriyaki sauce and stir-fry for 1 more minute.

6 Add the cooked noodles and cauliflower and cook for 1–2 minutes, stirring to coat in the sauce.

7 Sprinkle with the sesame seeds and serve immediately.

OR YOU CAN TRY THIS...
– Sprinkle with chopped coriander (cilantro).
– Add some thinly sliced green or yellow (bell) peppers or baby corn.

CLASSIC CAULIFLOWER CHEESE

SERVES: 3-4 | **PREP:** 10 MINUTES | **COOK:** 25-30 MINUTES

1 large cauliflower,
  trimmed, stem removed
  and separated into florets
75g/3oz (scant ½ cup)
  butter
50g/2oz (½ cup) plain
  (all-purpose) flour
500ml/17fl oz (generous
  2 cups) milk
200g/7oz (2 cups) grated
  Cheddar cheese, plus
  extra for sprinkling
1 tsp English or Dijon
  mustard
cayenne pepper, for dusting
sea salt and freshly ground
  black pepper

Comforting, homely and delicious, there's something very special about a classic baked cauliflower cheese. You can use a sharp, piquant Cheddar or a milder version, depending on your personal taste. And if you're counting the calories and watching your waistline, you could substitute reduced fat cheese and skimmed milk.

1 Preheat the oven to 190°C, 375°F, gas mark 5.

2 Bring a large pan of water to the boil and add the cauliflower florets. Boil for about 8 minutes, or until the cauliflower is just tender. Be careful not to overcook it or it will lose its shape and go mushy. Drain well and pat the cauliflower with kitchen paper (paper towels) to absorb the moisture.

3 Meanwhile, melt the butter in a pan over a low heat. Stir in the flour with a wooden spoon and cook for 2–3 minutes, stirring, until you have a smooth, nutty smelling paste. Gradually whisk in the milk, a little at a time, beating until it's all added and free of lumps. Turn up the heat and bring to the boil, stirring all the time, until it thickens and you have a smooth, glossy sauce. Reduce the heat to low and cook for 2–3 minutes.

4 Remove from the heat and stir in the grated Cheddar and mustard. Season to taste with salt and pepper.

5 Arrange the cauliflower in a large, shallow ovenproof dish and pour the sauce over the top to cover it completely. Sprinkle with extra grated cheese and dust with cayenne.

6 Bake in the oven for 15–20 minutes until piping hot and crisp and golden brown on top. Serve immediately.

OR YOU CAN TRY THIS...
– Use Caerphilly, Lancashire or Parmesan cheese.
– Sprinkle some fresh breadcrumbs over the top before baking.

SICILIAN CAULIFLOWER SALAD

SERVES: 4 | **PREP:** 15 MINUTES | **COOK:** 15 MINUTES

~~~~~~

1 medium cauliflower,
   trimmed, stem removed
   and separated into florets
a few saffron strands
6 tbsp olive oil
1 medium aubergine
   (eggplant), cubed
1 large onion, thinly sliced
a pinch of caster (superfine)
   sugar
50g/2oz (½ cup) pine nuts
50g/2oz (scant ½ cup)
   sultanas (golden raisins)
2 tbsp capers
1 red chilli, deseeded and
   diced
balsamic vinegar, for
   drizzling
a handful of flat-leaf parsley,
   finely chopped
3 tbsp grated Parmesan or
   Pecorino cheese
sea salt and freshly ground
   black pepper
crusty bread, to serve

Cooking the cauliflower with saffron gives it a lovely golden colour and adds a subtle flavour to this warm salad. The heat of the chilli complements the sweetness of the onions, sultanas and balsamic vinegar.

1 Cook the cauliflower florets with the saffron in a pan of boiling salted water for 4–5 minutes until just tender but still slightly crisp. Do not overcook it. Drain well and pat dry with kitchen paper (paper towels). Set aside to cool.

2 Meanwhile, heat 5 tablespoons of the oil in a large frying pan (skillet) over a medium heat and cook the aubergine, stirring occasionally, for 5 minutes, or until golden brown. Remove from the pan and drain on kitchen paper (paper towels).

3 Add the remaining oil to the pan together with the onion. Cook for 6–8 minutes, stirring occasionally, until tender, golden brown and starting to crisp and caramelise. Stir in the sugar, pine nuts, sultanas, capers and chilli. Cook for 1–2 minutes until the sultanas plump up and the pine nuts are golden. Stir in the aubergine and season to taste with salt and pepper.

4 Transfer to a serving bowl, then add the cauliflower and toss gently. Drizzle with a little balsamic vinegar and sprinkle with the parsley and cheese. Serve warm with crusty bread.

OR YOU CAN TRY THIS...
– Add some diced tomatoes or red (bell) pepper.
– Vary the herbs – try basil, mint or oregano.
– Add a good squeeze of lemon juice.

~~~~~~

CAULIFLOWER RICE SALAD WITH PUMPKIN & SPINACH

SERVES: 4 | **PREP:** 20 MINUTES | **COOK:** 35 MINUTES

500g/1¼lb pumpkin, peeled, deseeded and cubed

2 red onions, cut into wedges

4 tbsp olive oil

1 large cauliflower, trimmed, stem removed and separated into florets

2 tbsp pumpkin seeds

2 tbsp pine nuts

2 garlic cloves, crushed

1 tbsp black mustard seeds

a pinch of crushed dried chilli flakes

115g/4oz baby spinach

50g/2oz (¼ cup) sun-blush tomatoes, roughly chopped

juice of 1 lemon

sea salt and freshly ground black pepper

This delicious salad is packed with really nutritious, healthy seeds and vegetables. Although it's best served warm, it keeps well, covered in the fridge, and could be eaten cold for a packed lunch the following day.

1 Preheat the oven to 180°C, 350°F, gas mark 4.

2 Arrange the pumpkin cubes and red onion wedges on a baking (cookie) sheet. Drizzle with 3 tablespoons of the olive oil and season with salt and pepper. Roast for 25–30 minutes until tender.

3 Meanwhile, pulse the cauliflower florets in a food processor until they have the consistency of rice-sized 'grains'.

4 Place a dry frying pan (skillet) over a medium heat and toast the pumpkin seeds and pine nuts for 1–2 minutes, tossing them gently, until golden. Remove immediately.

5 Add the remaining olive oil to the pan and cook the garlic and mustard seeds for 2 minutes. Add the chilli flakes and cauliflower rice and cook for 4–5 minutes, stirring well, until the cauliflower is warm and tender but still slightly crunchy.

6 Transfer the 'rice' to a large serving bowl, then mix in the spinach and sun-blush tomatoes. Add the pumpkin, red onion wedges, toasted seeds and pine nuts. Toss gently together, then sprinkle with the lemon juice. Check the seasoning and serve the salad warm.

OR YOU CAN TRY THIS...

– Add some chopped parsley, mint, basil or coriander (cilantro).
– If you don't have sun-blush, use fresh cherry or baby plum tomatoes.
– Instead of pumpkin, use butternut squash or sweet potato.
– Stir in some sultanas (golden raisins), preserved lemon and cumin seeds.
– Add beans, chickpeas, tofu or halloumi.

CAULIFLOWER & QUINOA PATTIES

SERVES: 4 | **PREP:** 25 MINUTES | **CHILL:** 30 MINUTES | **COOK:** 25-35 MINUTES

1 small cauliflower,
   trimmed, stem removed
   and separated into florets
175g/6oz (1 cup) quinoa,
   rinsed and drained
115g/4oz (1 cup) grated
   Parmesan cheese
2 garlic cloves, crushed
4 spring onions (scallions),
   thinly sliced
75g/3oz (¾ cup) rolled oats
a bunch of flat-leaf parsley,
   chopped
grated zest of 1 lemon
3 medium free-range eggs,
   beaten
2 tbsp sunflower or light
   olive oil
sea salt and freshly ground
   black pepper
tzatziki, guacamole or pesto
   and crisp salad, to serve

These little patties can be prepared in advance and kept covered in the fridge until you're ready to cook them.

1 Pulse the cauliflower florets in a food processor until they have the consistency of small 'grains' of couscous.

2 Bring 475ml/16fl oz (2 cups) water to the boil in a pan and add the quinoa. Reduce the heat and simmer gently, covered, for 15 minutes, or until tender and most of the water has been absorbed. It's ready when the 'sprout' or 'tail' pops out of the seed. Turn off the heat and set aside for 6–8 minutes before draining off any excess liquid. Fluff the quinoa up with a fork.

3 Transfer the quinoa to a large bowl and stir in the cauliflower grains, cheese, garlic, spring onions, oats, parsley and lemon zest. Season with salt and pepper and add the beaten eggs. Stir until all the ingredients are thoroughly combined and you have a firm mixture. If it's too dry, moisten with a little water. Conversely, if it's too moist, add some more oats to firm it up.

4 Divide the mixture into 12 portions and shape each one into a patty. Chill in the fridge for 30 minutes before cooking.

5 Heat the oil in a large frying pan (skillet) set over a medium heat and fry the patties in batches, for 4–5 minutes on each side until heated right through, crisp and golden brown. Remove from the pan with a slotted spoon and drain on kitchen paper (paper towels).

6 Serve hot with some tzatziki, guacamole or pesto and a crisp salad.

OR YOU CAN TRY THIS...
– Use grated Cheddar, crumbled feta or goat's cheese instead of Parmesan.
– Use flour instead of oats to bind the mixture.
– Add some shredded kale or spinach.

CAULIFLOWER, LEEK & BACON GRATIN

SERVES: 4 | **PREP:** 20 MINUTES | **COOK:** 35-40 MINUTES

100g/3½oz (½ cup) cubed pancetta or bacon lardons

1 large cauliflower, trimmed, stem removed and separated into florets

2 leeks, trimmed and thickly sliced

75g/3oz (scant ½ cup) butter

50g/2oz (½ cup) plain (all-purpose) flour

500ml/17fl oz (generous 2 cups) milk

4 tbsp reduced fat crème fraîche

150g/5oz (1½ cups) grated Cheddar cheese

2 tsp wholegrain mustard

40g/1½oz (¾ cup) fresh breadcrumbs

sea salt and freshly ground black pepper

This creamy gratin has a delicious crispy topping of cheesy breadcrumbs. You can eat it with a crisp green salad or roasted tomatoes as a light meal or serve as an accompaniment to a baked gammon or roast chicken.

1 Preheat the oven to 200°C, 400°F, gas mark 6.

2 Cook the pancetta or bacon in a frying pan (skillet) over a medium heat for 8–10 minutes, or until crisp and golden brown all over. You don't need to use oil as the fat will run out of the bacon.

3 Cook the cauliflower florets and leeks in a large pan of salted boiling water for about 8 minutes, or until the vegetables are just tender. Drain well.

4 Meanwhile, melt the butter in a large pan over a low heat. Stir in the flour with a wooden spoon and cook for 2–3 minutes, stirring, until you have a smooth, nutty smelling paste. Gradually whisk in the milk, a little at a time, beating until it's all added and free of lumps. Turn up the heat and bring to the boil, stirring all the time, until it thickens and you have a smooth, glossy sauce. Reduce the heat to low and cook for 2–3 minutes. Remove from the heat and stir in the crème fraîche, three-quarters of the grated Cheddar and the mustard. Season to taste with salt and pepper.

5 Stir the cauliflower, leeks and bacon into the sauce and transfer to a large, shallow ovenproof dish. Sprinkle with the breadcrumbs and the remaining cheese. Cover with foil.

6 Bake in the oven for 15 minutes, then remove the foil and cook for a further 10–15 minutes until bubbling, crisp and golden brown.

OR YOU CAN TRY THIS...
– Add some sautéed button mushrooms or cherry tomatoes.
– Use Gruyère, Emmental, Parmesan or even smoked Cheddar.

CAULIFLOWER, FENNEL & POMEGRANATE SALAD

SERVES: 4 | **PREP:** 15 MINUTES | **COOK:** 15-20 MINUTES

1 medium cauliflower, trimmed, stem removed and separated into small florets
1 small fennel bulb, trimmed and thinly sliced (reserve the leafy fronds)
5 tbsp olive oil
1 tbsp cider vinegar
juice of ½ lemon
1 tsp wholegrain mustard
2 tsp clear honey
1 tsp cumin seeds
50g/2oz (generous ¼ cup) chopped toasted pistachios
a handful of dill, chopped
a handful of mint, chopped
seeds of 1 small pomegranate
sea salt and freshly ground black pepper

This is a great salad for chilly autumn and winter days when you don't feel like munching your way through salad leaves and tomatoes. The fennel adds crispness and a subtle aniseed flavour, while the sweet pomegranate seeds glow like rubies – a splash of bright colour contrasting with the creamy vegetables.

1 Preheat the oven to 220°C, 425°F, gas mark 7.

2 Toss the cauliflower and fennel in 3 tablespoons of the olive oil and spread them out in a single layer on a baking (cookie) sheet. Season with a little sea salt and pepper. Roast for about 15–20 minutes until just tender, golden brown and crisp at the edges.

3 In a large bowl, mix the remaining olive oil with the vinegar, lemon juice, mustard and honey until well combined. Add the warm roasted cauliflower and fennel and toss gently. Stir in the cumin seeds, pistachios, dill and mint. Finely chop any leftover feathery fennel fronds and add to the salad.

4 Sprinkle the pomegranate seeds over and finish with a grinding of sea salt. Serve warm.

OR YOU CAN TRY THIS...
– Use fennel seeds instead of cumin seeds.
– Try roasted pine nuts or hazelnuts instead of pistachios.
– Add some chopped red onion or spring onions (scallions).
– Substitute freshly squeezed orange juice for the lemon juice.
– Add a crushed garlic clove or some diced red chilli to the dressing.

CAULIFLOWER STEAKS WITH MEDITERRANEAN RELISH

SERVES: 4 | **PREP:** 15 MINUTES | **COOK:** 35-40 MINUTES

1 large cauliflower, stalk
   trimmed
3 tbsp olive oil
250g/9oz tomatoes,
   chopped
3 garlic cloves, crushed
a pinch of sugar
a splash of balsamic vinegar
sea salt and freshly ground
   black pepper

For the Mediterranean relish:
50g/2oz (½ cup) diced
   black olives (packed in
   oil, not brine)
¼ red onion, diced
1 small red chilli, deseeded
   and diced
2 sun-blush tomatoes, diced
a small handful of basil
   leaves, torn
1 tbsp fruity olive oil
a squeeze of lemon juice

Here's a lovely vegetarian dish for a light meal in summer. You don't have to serve it piping hot – it's equally good served lukewarm or at room temperature. Buy the best olives you can find for the relish – Greek Kalamata ones are especially good.

1 Preheat the oven to 200°C, 400°F, gas mark 6.

2 Mix all the relish ingredients together in a bowl and set aside.

3 Slice the cauliflower through the stem into 4 thick 'steaks'. Heat 1 tablespoon of the olive oil in a frying pan (skillet) set over a high heat. Add the cauliflower steaks, one at a time, to the hot pan and cook for 4 minutes, turning halfway through, until starting to colour. Place on a large baking (cookie) sheet and roast in the oven for 20 minutes, or until tender, golden brown and slightly charred.

4 Meanwhile, add the remaining oil to the frying pan and reduce the heat. Cook the tomatoes and garlic, stirring occasionally, for 5 minutes, or until tender, reduced and thickened. Stir in the sugar, balsamic and salt and pepper to taste. Blitz the tomato mixture in a blender or food processor until smooth.

5 Divide the tomato sauce between 4 serving plates, spreading it out in a circle. Place the roasted cauliflower steaks on top and top with the Mediterranean relish. Serve immediately.

OR YOU CAN TRY THIS...
– For the relish, use green olives, baby plum tomatoes, chopped mint and coriander (cilantro).
– Drizzle the cauliflower with some pesto.
– Use canned plum tomatoes instead of fresh tomatoes.

CAULIFLOWER SALAD WITH PRAWNS & DILL

SERVES: 4 | **PREP:** 15 MINUTES | **COOK:** 5-7 MINUTES

1 medium cauliflower, trimmed, stem removed and separated into florets
3 celery sticks, thinly sliced
4 spring onions (scallions), chopped
450g/1lb cooked shelled prawns (shrimp)
1 ripe avocado, peeled, stoned (pitted) and cubed
1 small bunch of dill, chopped
sea salt and freshly ground black pepper

For the creamy lemon dressing:
200g/7oz (scant 1 cup) 0% fat Greek yoghurt
2 tbsp light mayonnaise
grated zest and juice of ½ lemon
1 garlic clove, crushed

This pretty salad is a great way to serve cauliflower on a warm summer's day. It's healthy, carb-free, gluten-free, and by using yoghurt to make the dressing, low in fat too. You can use freshly cooked or frozen, defrosted prawns (shrimp).

1 Steam the cauliflower florets or cook in a pan of boiling salted water for 5–7 minutes until just tender but still slightly crisp. Take care not to overcook it – you want the florets to keep their shape. Drain well and pat dry with kitchen paper (paper towels). Set aside to cool.

2 Mix all the dressing ingredients together in a bowl. Season to taste with salt and pepper.

3 When the cauliflower is cool, put it in a large bowl with the celery, spring onions, prawns and avocado. Add most of the dill and toss gently in the dressing.

4 Check the seasoning, adding more salt and pepper if needed. Sprinkle with the remaining dill and serve.

OR YOU CAN TRY THIS...
– Use crab meat instead of prawns.
– Mash the avocado and mix it into the dressing.
– Add some steamed asparagus tips, thin green beans or peas.
– Substitute chopped parsley or coriander (cilantro) for the dill.
– For a more substantial meal, add some cooked pasta shapes.

CAULIFLOWER & HALLOUMI TRAYBAKE

SERVES: 4 | **PREP:** 15 MINUTES | **COOK:** 35 MINUTES

1 large cauliflower,
   stalk trimmed
1 tsp ground coriander
1 tsp ground cumin
1 tsp ground cinnamon
½ tsp ground turmeric
4 tbsp olive oil
2 red onions, cut into wedges
150g/5oz cherry tomatoes
250g/9oz halloumi, sliced
pomegranate molasses,
   for drizzling
sea salt and freshly ground
   black pepper
couscous, quinoa or rice,
   to serve

A traybake is a really quick and easy meal. Roasted thick slices of cauliflower ('steaks') are surprisingly filling and cooking them with halloumi is a great combo.

1 Preheat the oven to 200°C, 400°F, gas mark 6.

2 Slice the cauliflower, through the stem, into 4 thick 'steaks'. Mix the spices with half the olive oil and brush over the cauliflower.

3 Arrange the cauliflower steaks in a large roasting tin with the onion wedges and tomatoes. Drizzle the remaining olive oil over the onions and tomatoes, and season lightly with salt and pepper.

4 Bake for 30 minutes, or until the vegetables are tender and the cauliflower is golden brown around the edges.

5 Preheat the grill (broiler) to high. Add the halloumi to the roasting tin and grill (broil) for at least 5 minutes until the cheese is hot and golden brown.

6 Drizzle with pomegranate molasses and serve with couscous, quinoa or rice.

OR YOU CAN TRY THIS...
– Brush the cauliflower steaks with some curry paste.
– Vary the vegetables – try beetroot (beets), pumpkin, red (bell) peppers or aubergine (eggplant).
– Mix in some drained, canned chickpeas or beans, shredded spinach or kale.
– Drizzle with pesto or balsamic vinegar.

SPICY INDIAN CAULIFLOWER SOUP

SERVES: 4 | **PREP:** 15 MINUTES | **COOK:** 30-35 MINUTES

2 tbsp vegetable oil, e.g. sunflower
1 large onion, chopped
3 garlic cloves, crushed
1 tbsp grated fresh root ginger
1 green chilli, shredded
2 tsp ground turmeric
1 tsp garam masala
2 tsp black mustard seeds
2 tsp cumin seeds
1 large cauliflower, trimmed and cut into chunks
1 large potato, peeled and diced
900ml/1½ pints (3¾ cups) hot vegetable stock
250ml/8fl oz (1 cup) reduced fat coconut milk
sea salt and freshly ground black pepper
yoghurt, chopped coriander (cilantro) and pumpkin seeds, to garnish

This spicy golden soup is easy to make, tastes delicious and freezes well, so you can make double the quantity and freeze a batch for a future date. Use dairy-free soya or coconut milk yoghurt alternative, to garnish, if you're vegan.

1 Heat the oil in a large pan and cook the onion, garlic and ginger over a medium heat, stirring occasionally, for 6–8 minutes until softened. Stir in the chilli, ground spices and seeds. Cook for 2 minutes until they release their aromas.

2 Stir in the cauliflower, potato and hot stock. Bring to the boil, then reduce the heat and simmer gently for 15–20 minutes, or until the vegetables are cooked and tender. Stir in the coconut milk and season to taste with salt and pepper.

3 Blitz the soup, in batches, in a food processor or blender until smooth. Return to the pan and heat through gently without boiling.

4 Ladle the soup into bowls and top with a spoonful of yoghurt and sprinkle with the chopped coriander and pumpkin seeds. Serve immediately.

OR YOU CAN TRY THIS...

– Add some carrots, sweet potato or pumpkin.
– Use cucumber raita instead of yoghurt as a topping.
– Fry some thinly sliced cauliflower florets in oil to use as a garnish.

THAI CAULIFLOWER & NOODLE SALAD

SERVES: 4 | **PREP:** 20 MINUTES | **COOK:** 15 MINUTES

1–2 tbsp vegetable oil, e.g. sunflower, plus extra for oiling
1 medium cauliflower, trimmed, stem removed and separated into small florets
150g/5oz rice vermicelli noodles
2 large carrots, thinly shredded
1 bunch of spring onions (scallions), diagonally sliced
½ cucumber, cut into matchstick strips
a handful of coriander (cilantro), chopped
50g/2oz (scant ½ cup) unsalted peanuts, toasted and chopped

For the dressing:
juice of 2 limes
4 tbsp nam pla (Thai fish sauce)
1 tbsp palm sugar
1 red bird's eye chilli, diced
1 garlic clove, crushed

This colourful salad has a fresh zingy flavour and even if you're not a great fan of salads you're sure to enjoy this. We've roasted the cauliflower for more taste and crunch but you could steam or boil it briefly instead.

1 Preheat the oven to 200°C, 400°F, gas mark 6. Lightly oil a baking (cookie) sheet.

2 Cut the cauliflower florets into smaller bite-sized pieces and arrange in a single layer on the baking sheet. Drizzle with the oil and bake for 15 minutes, or until the cauliflower is tender but still retains a little bite. Leave to cool.

3 Meanwhile, soak the rice noodles following the pack instructions. Drain.

4 Whisk all the dressing ingredients together in a small bowl.

5 Put the cauliflower, carrots, spring onions and cucumber into a large bowl. Add the drained noodles, coriander and dressing and toss everything gently together to coat in the dressing.

6 Serve the salad sprinkled with chopped peanuts.

OR YOU CAN TRY THIS...

– Add some thinly sliced red or yellow (bell) peppers.
– Stir a little peanut butter or grated fresh root ginger into the dressing.
– Substitute mint or Thai basil for coriander.
– To make the salad more substantial you could add some shredded chicken or prawns (shrimp).

MAIN MEALS

MOROCCAN SPICED VEGETABLES WITH COUSCOUS

SERVES: 4 | **PREP:** 20 MINUTES | **COOK:** 25-30 MINUTES

1 medium cauliflower, stem removed and cut into florets
1 red onion, cut into wedges
1 red (bell) pepper, deseeded and cut into chunks
1 aubergine (eggplant), trimmed and cubed
4 tbsp olive oil
1 tsp ground cumin
1 tsp ground coriander
a good pinch of ground cinnamon
sea salt and freshly ground black pepper
hot sauce or pomegranate molasses, for drizzling

For the couscous:
200g/7oz (generous 1 cup) couscous
240ml/8fl oz (1 cup) hot vegetable stock
3 tbsp olive oil
50g/2oz (scant ½ cup) sultanas (golden raisins), soaked (see Tip)
a handful of flat-leaf parsley, chopped
a handful of mint, chopped
juice of 1 large lemon
1 tbsp tahini
seeds of ½ pomegranate

You can serve this couscous with gently spiced vegetables warm or cold as a substantial summer salad. The roast cauliflower adds crispness and crunch.

1 Preheat the oven to 200°C, 400°F, gas mark 6.

2 Put the vegetables, olive oil and spices in a large bowl and toss to coat. Season lightly with salt and pepper. Spread them out on a large baking (cookie) sheet and roast for 25–30 minutes until tender and starting to char. Turn them halfway through.

3 Meanwhile, put the couscous in a bowl and pour the vegetable stock and olive oil over the top. Cover the bowl and leave for 12–15 minutes until the couscous swells and absorbs the liquid. Fluff it up with a fork.

4 Stir the sultanas, herbs, lemon juice, tahini and pomegranate seeds into the couscous. Season to taste with salt and pepper.

5 Divide the couscous between 4 serving plates and top with the roasted vegetables. Drizzle with hot sauce or pomegranate molasses and serve warm.

OR YOU CAN TRY THIS...
– Add some toasted pine nuts, pistachios or pumpkin seeds.
– Serve with a bowl of chilled yoghurt or tzatziki.

TIP: To soak the sultanas, pour some boiling water over them and leave for 10 minutes until plumped up and softened. Drain well.

CAULIFLOWER & LENTIL PILAF

SERVES: 4 | **PREP:** 15 MINUTES | **COOK:** 30-35 MINUTES

1 medium cauliflower, trimmed, stem removed and separated into small florets
1 sweet potato, peeled and cut into small chunks
2 tsp fennel seeds
½ tsp ground turmeric
2 tbsp vegetable oil
2 spring onions (scallions), diced
juice of 1 lemon
sea salt and freshly ground black pepper

For the lentil pilaf:
2 tbsp vegetable oil
1 large onion, diced
2 garlic cloves, crushed
1–2 tbsp curry paste (depending on how hot you like it)
1 tbsp black mustard seeds
seeds from 4 cardamom pods
100g/3½oz (½ cup) red lentils
840ml/28fl oz (3½ cups) hot vegetable stock
200g/7oz (scant 1 cup) basmati rice
a handful of coriander (cilantro), chopped

This healthy pilaf is packed with nutrients and makes a warming supper dish on cold winter days. And it's low fat and vegan-friendly.

1 Preheat the oven to 200°C, 400°F, gas mark 6.

2 Put the cauliflower florets and potato chunks in a large bowl and toss with the fennel seeds, turmeric and oil. Season lightly with salt and pepper, then spread them out on a large baking (cookie) sheet and roast for 25–30 minutes until tender and starting to char. Turn them halfway through.

3 Make the lentil pilaf: heat the vegetable oil in a large pan set over a medium heat and cook the onion and garlic, stirring occasionally, for 5 minutes, or until tender. Stir in the curry paste and seeds and cook for 1 minute. Add the lentils together with the hot stock, then turn up the heat and bring to the boil. Reduce the heat to low and simmer gently for 10 minutes.

4 Stir the rice into the lentils, cover the pan and simmer gently for 15 minutes, or until the lentils and rice are cooked and have absorbed the stock. Stir in the coriander.

5 Divide the lentil pilaf between 4 shallow serving bowls and serve with the roasted vegetables piled on top. Sprinkle with the spring onions and drizzle with the lemon juice.

OR YOU CAN TRY THIS...
– Vary the vegetables: roast some carrots, parsnips, pumpkin or squash.
– Instead of stock, use reduced fat coconut milk.

ROAST CHICKEN & CAULIFLOWER TRAYBAKE

SERVES: 4 | **PREP:** 15 MINUTES | **COOK:** 40 MINUTES

4 boneless chicken breasts (skin on)
1 medium cauliflower, trimmed, stem removed and separated into small florets
400g/14oz baby new potatoes
2 red onions, cut into wedges
8 unpeeled garlic cloves
sprigs of rosemary and oregano
juice of 1 large lemon
fruity green olive oil, for drizzling
3 tbsp grated Cheddar or Parmesan cheese
sea salt and freshly ground black pepper
green salad, to serve

One-pan meals are so easy to make and cut down on washing up. What's not to like? This traybake is perfect for a no-fuss supper when you get home from work.

1 Preheat the oven to 200°C, 400°F, gas mark 6.

2 Arrange the chicken breasts (skin side up), cauliflower florets, potatoes and onions in a single layer in a large roasting tin. Tuck the garlic cloves and herb sprigs into the gaps between them. Pour the lemon juice over the top and drizzle with plenty of olive oil. Season with salt and pepper.

3 Roast for 40 minutes, turning the chicken and vegetables two or three times, so they cook evenly and colour on both sides.

4 About 10 minutes before the end of the cooking time, remove the tin from the oven and sprinkle the cheese over the top. Continue roasting until the cheese has melted, the vegetables are tender and the chicken is thoroughly cooked, crisp and golden brown.

5 Squeeze the garlic out of the skins and mash into the pan juices. Discard any charred herbs. Serve the hot cheesy chicken and vegetables with a crisp green salad.

OR YOU CAN TRY THIS...

– Try adding sweet potato chunks, aubergine (eggplant), red, yellow or green (bell) peppers and cherry tomatoes.
– Use chicken wings or thighs instead of breasts.
– Use tofu or halloumi instead of chicken.
– Stir in some spinach or shredded kale when you add the cheese.

CRISPY SALMON & CAULIFLOWER BAKE

SERVES: 4 | **PREP:** 10 MINUTES | **COOK:** 35 MINUTES

4 thick salmon fillets,
   skinned
1 small cauliflower,
   trimmed, stem removed
   and separated into florets
100g/3½oz (1 cup)
   cooked peas
1 medium free-range egg
2 tsp Dijon mustard
300g/11oz (1¼ cups) Greek
   yoghurt
grated zest of 1 lemon
6 tbsp fresh white
   breadcrumbs
cayenne pepper, for dusting
sea salt and freshly ground
   black pepper

This delicious crispy bake is delicious and nutritious – a great way to get your omega-3 fatty acids for heart health. We've used a low fat yoghurt sauce but you could substitute a more traditional white béchamel sauce made with flour, butter and milk.

1 Preheat the oven to 200°C, 400°F, gas mark 6.

2 Place the salmon fillets in a large deep frying pan (skillet) or sauté pan and cover them with cold water. Cover with a lid and bring to the boil. Reduce the heat immediately to a simmer and cook gently for 10 minutes, or until tender and cooked through.

3 With a slotted spoon or fish slice, lift the salmon out of the poaching liquid and flake it into large pieces with a fork. Transfer to a large shallow ovenproof dish.

4 While the salmon is poaching, cook the cauliflower florets in a pan of boiling salted water for about 5 minutes until just tender. Drain well and pat dry with kitchen paper (paper towels). Add to the salmon in the dish along with the peas.

5 Beat together the egg, mustard, yoghurt and lemon zest in a bowl. Season with a little salt and pepper and drizzle over the salmon and vegetables to coat them. Sprinkle the breadcrumbs over the top and dust with cayenne.

6 Bake for 20 minutes, or until set and golden brown and the breadcrumbs are crisp.

OR YOU CAN TRY THIS...
– Add some broccoli florets.
– Use canned salmon instead of fresh.
– Top with some grated Cheddar.
– Mix in some cooked pasta shapes for a more substantial dish.

CAULIFLOWER SPAGHETTI CARBONARA

SERVES: 4 | **PREP:** 10 MINUTES | **COOK:** 10 MINUTES

500g/1¼lb spaghetti
1 medium cauliflower,
    trimmed, stem removed
    and separated into florets
200g/7oz (1 cup) cubed
    pancetta
2 garlic cloves, crushed
2 medium free-range eggs
1 medium free-range
    egg yolk
100ml/3½fl oz (scant
    ½ cup) reduced fat
    crème fraîche
100g/3½oz (scant 1 cup)
    grated Parmesan cheese
a small handful of flat-leaf
    parsley, finely chopped
sea salt and freshly ground
    black pepper

A mound of creamy spaghetti carbonara is comfort food at its very best. Adding cauliflower to this classic Roman dish not only makes it more filling but also enhances its flavour and texture. Quick and easy to make, it's a great weekday supper.

1 Cook the spaghetti in a large pan following the pack instructions. Add the cauliflower florets to the pan for the last 4–5 minutes of cooking time, by which time they should be slightly tender (*al dente*). Drain well.

2 Meanwhile, cook the pancetta in a frying pan (skillet) set over a medium to high heat, stirring occasionally, until crisp and golden brown – there's no need to use oil as the fat will run out of the pancetta. Add the garlic for the last minute or two. Remove and drain on kitchen paper (paper towels).

3 In a bowl, beat together the eggs, egg yolk, crème fraîche and most of the Parmesan. Season lightly with salt and pepper.

4 Return the drained spaghetti and cauliflower to the hot large pan and stir in the egg mixture and pancetta. Add the parsley and toss everything gently together. The heat from the pasta will cook the eggs so you end up with a creamy sauce.

5 Divide between 4 shallow serving bowls and sprinkle with the remaining Parmesan and lots of black pepper.

OR YOU CAN TRY THIS...
– Use bacon lardons if you don't have pancetta.
– You can use double (heavy) cream but it is very rich.
– Try Pecorino or Grana Padano instead of Parmesan.
– Add some peas or mushrooms.
– Use any long pasta: linguine, tagliatelle or pappardelle.

CAULIFLOWER PIZZA WITH TOMATO CRUDO & ROCKET

SERVES: 4 | **PREP:** 10 MINUTES | **DRAIN:** 10-15 MINUTES | **COOK:** 35 MINUTES

1 large cauliflower,
   trimmed, stem removed
   and separated into florets
115g/4oz (½ cup) cream
   cheese or chevre goat's
   cheese
1 garlic clove, crushed
a pinch of dried oregano
1 large free-range egg,
   beaten
a handful of fresh rocket
   (arugula) leaves
good-quality balsamic
   vinegar, for drizzling
shaved Parmesan cheese,
   for sprinkling
sea salt and freshly ground
   black pepper

For the tomato crudo topping:
450g/1lb large ripe, fragrant
   tomatoes
1 garlic clove, crushed
a small handful of basil
   leaves, chopped
2 tsp fruity green olive oil

To make the topping for this summer pizza you'll need the most fragrant ripe tomatoes, not the insipid packaged ones on the shelves of many supermarkets, which have no aroma or flavour. Sniff before you buy! Look for varieties such as Marmande and don't worry if they are misshapen – farmers' markets are a good place to find them.

1 Preheat the oven to 200°C, 400°F, gas mark 6. Line a large baking (cookie) sheet with baking parchment.

2 Put the cauliflower florets in a food processor and pulse until they have the consistency of 'crumbs'. Transfer to a glass bowl, cover with clingfilm (plastic wrap) and microwave on high for 3–4 minutes. Spoon the cauliflower on to a stack of kitchen paper (paper towels) or a clean tea towel and press out any liquid until the grains are dry.

3 Mix the cauliflower in a large bowl with the cream cheese, garlic, oregano, beaten egg and salt and pepper until it sticks together. If it's too dry, moisten with a little water or olive oil.

4 Place on the lined baking sheet and, using your hands, flatten and stretch the mixture until you have a large circle about 1cm/½in thick. Bake for 30 minutes, or until crisp and golden brown.

5 For the topping, skin the tomatoes by plunging them into boiling water and then slipping off the skins. Cut each tomato in half and scoop out and discard the seeds. Put the tomatoes, cut side down, in a colander and leave to drain for 10–15 minutes, then cut them into dice. Mix with the garlic, basil and olive oil and season with salt and pepper.

6 Spoon the tomato mixture over the cooked pizza crust and pile the rocket on top. Drizzle with balsamic vinegar and sprinkle with the Parmesan shavings. Cut into wedges to serve.

ITALIAN WHOLE ROASTED CAULIFLOWER CHEESE

SERVES: 4 | **PREP:** 10 MINUTES | **COOK:** 30-35 MINUTES

1 large cauliflower, stem trimmed
olive oil for brushing
1 medium free-range egg, beaten
50g/2oz (½ cup) grated Parmesan cheese
paprika or cayenne pepper, for dusting

For the cheesy sauce:
2 tbsp olive oil
1 bunch of spring onions (scallions), thinly sliced
1 garlic clove, crushed
6 tbsp dry white vermouth, e.g. Martini Bianco or Noilly Prat
120ml/4fl oz (½ cup) reduced fat crème fraîche
200g/7oz (2 cups) grated Parmesan cheese
a handful of finely chopped flat-leaf parsley
1 bunch of chives, snipped
sea salt and freshly ground black pepper

A whole roasted cauliflower always looks impressive. This recipe is a different take on the traditional baked cauliflower cheese and elevates it into a delicious dish for a special occasion.

1 Preheat the oven to 200°C, 400°F, gas mark 6.

2 Cook the whole cauliflower in a large deep pan of simmering salted water for 15–20 minutes, or until it is just tender. Lift out of the pan and drain in a colander. Cool a little and pat dry with kitchen paper (paper towels).

3 Lightly brush a roasting tin with oil and place the cauliflower, stem down, in it. Brush the beaten egg over the top and sides and sprinkle with grated Parmesan. Cook in the preheated oven for 15 minutes, or until the cauliflower is crisp and golden all over.

4 While the cauliflower is cooking, make the cheesy sauce: heat the oil in a frying pan (skillet) over a low to medium heat and cook the spring onions and garlic for 4–5 minutes until softened. Pour in the vermouth and let it bubble away, stirring occasionally, until it reduces.

5 Reduce the heat to low and add the crème fraîche and Parmesan. Stir gently until all the cheese has melted and the sauce is smooth. Add the herbs and seasoning, to taste.

6 Serve the cauliflower cut into slices, dusted with paprika or cayenne and drizzled with the cheesy sauce.

OR YOU CAN TRY THIS...
– Use grated Cheddar, Emmental, Mahon or Monterrey Jack cheese instead of Parmesan.
– If you don't have white vermouth, a medium or dry white wine is fine.

INDIAN SPICED CAULIFLOWER PULAO

SERVES: 4 | **PREP:** 15 MINUTES | **COOK:** 1 HOUR | **STAND:** 10-15 MINUTES

4 tbsp vegetable oil

2 large onions, thinly sliced

3 garlic cloves, crushed

2.5cm/1in piece fresh root
   ginger, peeled and diced

2 red chillies, diced

1 tsp cumin seeds

1 tsp crushed coriander
   seeds

1 tsp ground turmeric

1 tsp garam masala

a pinch of ground cloves

400g/14oz can chickpeas,
   rinsed and drained

3 tomatoes, skinned and
   chopped

1 small cauliflower,
   trimmed, stem removed
   and separated into small
   florets

115g/4oz (scant 1 cup) fresh
   or frozen peas

600ml/1 pint (2½ cups)
   vegetable stock

juice of 1 lime

225g/8oz (1 cup) basmati
   rice

4 tablespoons plain yoghurt

a handful of coriander
   (cilantro), chopped

sea salt and freshly ground
   black pepper

Cauliflower is the main ingredient in many Indian curries and rice dishes. It holds its shape well and absorbs the spices and their colour. This pulao is a meal in itself but you can serve it with a traditional Indian salad of chopped tomatoes, red onion, cucumber, chilli and lemon or lime juice (kachumber).

1 Heat the oil in a large saucepan set over a low heat. Cook the onions, stirring occasionally, for 10–15 minutes until really tender and golden. Stir in the garlic and ginger and cook for 2–3 minutes.

2 Turn up the heat to medium and add the chillies, seeds and spices. Cook for 5 minutes, then stir in the chickpeas and tomatoes. Cook for 5 minutes and stir in the cauliflower and peas. Add the stock and lime juice and simmer gently for 5 minutes.

3 Stir in the rice and cook for 10 minutes, then reduce the heat, cover the pan and simmer gently for 15 minutes, or until the rice has absorbed most of the stock. Remove from the heat and set aside for 10–15 minutes.

4 Stir in the yoghurt and season to taste with salt and pepper. Divide between 4 shallow bowls and sprinkle with the coriander.

OR YOU CAN TRY THIS...

– Vary the vegetables: try carrots, potatoes or sweet potatoes instead of chickpeas.

– Add some red or green (bell) peppers, spinach or thin green beans.

– Serve with some cooling cucumber raita or a spicy chutney or relish.

ANDALUSIAN CAULIFLOWER RICE PAELLA

SERVES: 4 | **PREP:** 15 MINUTES | **COOK:** 20 MINUTES

1 medium cauliflower, trimmed, stem removed and separated into florets

175g/6oz (¾ cup) cubed chorizo

2 red or green (bell) peppers, deseeded and chopped

1 small red onion, diced

2 garlic cloves, crushed

1 tbsp olive oil

½ tsp ground cumin

a good pinch of smoked paprika

350g/12oz shelled raw large prawns (jumbo shrimp)

a handful of flat-leaf parsley, chopped

juice of 1 lemon

salt and freshly ground black pepper

This easy no-carb version of a Spanish paella is so simple and tastes deliciously hot and spicy. You can use defrosted prawns (shrimp) – keep a bag in your freezer just in case.

1 Put the cauliflower florets in a food processor and pulse until they have the consistency of rice-sized 'grains'.

2 In a large deep frying pan (skillet) set over a medium heat, cook the chorizo, stirring often, until it's golden brown and crisp and the fat runs out of it. Add the peppers, onion and garlic and cook for 4–5 minutes until just tender.

3 Add the olive oil, spices and cauliflower and cook for 4–5 minutes, stirring occasionally, until the 'rice' is warm and tender but still slightly crunchy.

4 Stir in the prawns and cook, stirring, for 2–3 minutes until they turn pink on both sides.

5 Season to taste with salt and pepper and stir in the parsley. Divide between 4 serving bowls and squeeze a little lemon juice over the top.

OR YOU CAN TRY THIS...

– For extra heat and spice, add some chilli powder or crushed dried chilli flakes.

– Substitute coriander (cilantro) for the parsley and use lime instead of lemon juice.

JAMAICAN JERK CAULIFLOWER STEAKS

SERVES: 4 | **PREP:** 10 MINUTES | **COOK:** 35-40 MINUTES

1 large cauliflower, stalk
 trimmed
2 tbsp jerk paste
juice of 1 lime
½ tbsp soy sauce
200g/7oz (scant 1 cup)
 long grain rice
200ml/7fl oz (scant 1 cup)
 reduced fat coconut milk
400g/14oz can kidney
 beans, rinsed and drained
1 bunch of spring onions
 (scallions), diced
sea salt and freshly ground
 black pepper
lime wedges, to serve

These spicy roast cauliflower steaks are served with the traditional Jamaican rice and 'peas', cooked in coconut milk. The peas are not the usual fresh green garden or frozen peas but canned red kidney beans.

1 Preheat the oven to 200°C, 400°F, gas mark 6. Line a baking (cookie) sheet with foil.

2 Cut the cauliflower head down through the stalk into 4 thick slices. Mix the jerk paste with the lime juice and soy sauce and brush over the cauliflower steaks. Arrange on the foil-lined baking sheet and bake for 35–40 minutes until tender, golden brown and slightly charred.

3 Cook the rice in the coconut milk and 200ml/7fl oz (scant 1 cup) water, following the pack instructions. When the rice is cooked and tender and has absorbed all the liquid, stir in the beans and spring onions. Season to taste with salt and pepper.

4 Serve the hot cauliflower steaks with the coconut rice and some lime wedges on the side, for squeezing.

OR YOU CAN TRY THIS...

– Use jerk seasoning, instead of paste, and mix it with the soy sauce and some tomato ketchup to coat the cauliflower.
– Add some diced hot red chilli or chopped coriander (cilantro) to the coconut rice.
– Use canned black beans instead of red kidney beans.

CAULIFLOWER, LEEK & MUSHROOM CRUMBLE

SERVES: 4 | **PREP:** 15 MINUTES | **COOK:** 35 MINUTES

1 small cauliflower, trimmed, stem removed and separated into florets

4 leeks, trimmed and thickly sliced

2 tbsp olive oil

350g/12oz chestnut mushrooms, thickly sliced

100g/3½oz (2 cups) fresh white breadcrumbs

a handful of flat-leaf parsley, finely chopped

sea salt and freshly ground black pepper

This savoury crumble is a variation on the classic cauliflower cheese and, with its crisp golden topping, it makes an easy supper dish. If you're in a hurry and don't have much time to cook, you can cheat and use ready-made cheese sauce.

1 Preheat the oven to 200°C, 400°F, gas mark 6.

2 Cook the cauliflower florets and leeks in a pan of boiling salted water for 5–6 minutes, or until just tender. Drain well and pat dry with kitchen paper (paper towels).

3 Meanwhile, heat the oil in a frying pan (skillet) set over a medium heat and cook the mushrooms, stirring occasionally, for 5 minutes, or until golden brown. Transfer to a shallow ovenproof dish and add the cauliflower and leeks.

4 Add the breadcrumbs to the hot frying pan and cook, stirring for 2–3 minutes until crisp and golden. Stir in the parsley and remove from the heat.

5 Meanwhile, make the cheese sauce: melt the butter in a pan set over a low heat. Stir in the flour and cook for 2–3 minutes, stirring, until you have a smooth paste. Gradually whisk in the milk, a little at a time, beating until it's all added and free of lumps. Bring to the boil, stirring all the time, until it thickens and is smooth and glossy. Reduce the heat to low and cook for 2–3 minutes. Off the heat, stir in the grated cheese and mustard. Season to taste with nutmeg, salt and pepper.

For the cheese sauce:
75g/3oz (scant ½ cup)
    butter
50g/2oz (½ cup) plain
    (all-purpose) flour
600ml/1 pint (2½ cups)
    milk
200g/7oz (2 cups) grated
    Cheddar cheese
1 tsp English or Dijon
    mustard
a good pinch of grated
    nutmeg

6 Pour the sauce over the vegetables to coat and then sprinkle with the herby breadcrumbs.

7 Bake in the preheated oven for 15 minutes, or until the sauce is bubbling and the topping is really crisp.

OR YOU CAN TRY THIS...
– Use broccoli instead of cauliflower or half and half.
– Parmesan, Emmental and Gruyère cheese all work well.
– Reserve a little grated cheese to sprinkle over the top before baking.

SICILIAN LINGUINE & CAULIFLOWER

SERVES: 4 | **PREP:** 10 MINUTES | **COOK:** 20 MINUTES

2 tbsp olive oil

3 onions, thinly sliced

3 garlic cloves, crushed

1 red chilli, deseeded
 and diced

1 tsp caster (superfine) sugar

a few drops of balsamic
 vinegar

1 small cauliflower,
 trimmed, stem removed
 and separated into florets

500g/1¼lb linguine

3 tbsp pine nuts

3 tbsp capers, drained

1 bunch of flat-leaf parsley,
 chopped

sea salt and freshly ground
 black pepper

grated Parmesan cheese,
 for serving

This tasty pasta dish includes sweet and sour (*agrodolce*) vegetables which are a characteristic of Sicilian cooking. For the best flavour, use a good-quality syrupy balsamic vinegar.

1 Heat the oil in a large frying pan (skillet) set over a low heat. Cook the onions, stirring occasionally for about 15 minutes, or until really soft and starting to colour. Add the garlic and chilli and cook for 2–3 minutes, then stir in the sugar and balsamic vinegar.

2 Meanwhile, cook the cauliflower florets in a pan of boiling salted water for 4–5 minutes, or until just tender but still *al dente*. Drain well and pat dry with kitchen paper (paper towels).

3 Cook the linguine following the pack instructions. Drain well and return to the pan. Stir in the onion mixture, cauliflower, pine nuts, capers and parsley. Season to taste with salt and pepper.

4 Divide between 4 shallow serving bowls and serve sprinkled with Parmesan.

OR YOU CAN TRY THIS...

– Substitute tagliatelle, fettuccine or spaghetti for the linguine.
– Add some grated lemon or orange zest.
– Steam or roast the cauliflower instead of boiling it.

CAULIFLOWER MAC & CHEESE WITH GREENS

SERVES: 4 | **PREP:** 15 MINUTES | **COOK:** 25-30 MINUTES

225g/8oz (2¼ cups)
  macaroni
1 medium cauliflower,
  trimmed, stem removed
  and separated into florets
75g/3oz (scant ½ cup)
  butter
50g/2oz (½ cup) plain
  (all-purpose) flour
500ml/17fl oz (generous
  2 cups) milk
1 tsp English or Dijon
  mustard
200g/7oz (2 cups) grated
  Parmesan cheese
75g/3oz spinach, trimmed
  and coarsely shredded
sea salt and freshly ground
  black pepper

Adding pasta and green vegetables to a cauliflower cheese transforms it into a filling supper. We've used grated Parmesan to give it a real Italian flavour.

1 Preheat the oven to 190°C, 375°F, gas mark 5.

2 Cook the macaroni following the pack instructions. Drain.

3 Cook the cauliflower in a large pan of boiling water for 6–8 minutes, or until just tender. Drain well and pat with kitchen paper (paper towels) to absorb the moisture.

4 Meanwhile, melt the butter in a pan over a low heat. Stir in the flour with a wooden spoon and cook for 2–3 minutes, stirring, until you have a smooth, nutty smelling paste. Gradually whisk in the milk, a little at a time, beating until it's all added and free of lumps. Turn up the heat and bring to the boil, stirring all the time, until it thickens and you have a smooth, glossy sauce. Reduce the heat to low and cook for 2–3 minutes.

5 Remove the pan from the heat and stir in the mustard and most of the Parmesan. Stir in the spinach and season to taste with salt and pepper.

6 Put the macaroni and cauliflower in a large shallow ovenproof dish, pour the sauce over the top and stir to coat the macaroni in the sauce. Sprinkle with the remaining Parmesan and bake for 15–20 minutes until piping hot and crisp and golden brown. Serve immediately.

OR YOU CAN TRY THIS...
– Use shredded kale instead of spinach.
– Add some broccoli, green beans or peas.
– Use grated Cheddar instead of Parmesan.

GREEK CAULIFLOWER SPANAKORIZO

SERVES: 4 | **PREP:** 10 MINUTES | **COOK:** 30 MINUTES

5 tbsp olive oil, plus extra for oiling

1 medium cauliflower, trimmed, stem removed and separated into florets

1 large onion, finely chopped

2 garlic cloves, crushed

250g/9oz (1½ cups) risotto rice e.g. Arborio or Carnaroli

1.2 litres/2 pints (5 cups) simmering vegetable stock

450g/1lb baby spinach

115g/4oz feta cheese, crumbled

1 small bunch of dill, chopped

grated zest and juice of 1 lemon

4 sprigs of cherry tomatoes on the vine

sea salt and freshly ground black pepper

Spanakorizo is the Greek equivalent of risotto – a comforting mixture of rice and spinach flavoured with dill. Keep a pan of vegetable stock simmering on the hob while you make it. You can't rush this dish – just keep adding the stock, a little at a time, and stir until it has been absorbed and the rice is cooked and tender.

1 Preheat the oven to 200°C, 400°F, gas mark 6. Lightly oil a baking (cookie) sheet.

2 Cut the cauliflower florets into smaller bite-sized pieces and arrange in a single layer on the baking sheet. Drizzle with 2 tablespoons of the oil and bake in the oven for 15–20 minutes, or until the cauliflower is tender but still retains a little bite. Leave to cool.

3 Meanwhile, heat 3 tablespoons of oil in a deep frying pan (skillet) over a low heat and cook the onion and garlic, stirring occasionally, for 10 minutes, or until softened but not coloured. Add the rice and stir for 1–2 minutes until glistening with oil and starting to crackle. Add a ladleful of the simmering stock and keep stirring until all the liquid has been absorbed. Continue doing this for 15 minutes, adding the stock a ladleful at a time, or until the risotto is cooked and *al dente* – the rice grains should be plump and tender but still slightly firm, not mushy.

4 Stir in the spinach and let it wilt into the rice. Add the feta, dill and lemon zest and juice. Season to taste and remove from the heat. Set aside to rest for 5 minutes.

5 Cook the tomatoes on a griddle (grill) pan brushed with oil, over a medium to high heat for 4–5 minutes until they start to soften and char.

6 Serve the risotto in shallow bowls topped with the roasted cauliflower and tomatoes.

CAULIFLOWER SCHNITZEL WITH MUSHROOM SAUCE

SERVES: 4 | **PREP:** 15 MINUTES | **COOK:** 30 MINUTES

1 large cauliflower,
    stalk trimmed
50g/2oz (½ cup) cornflour
    (cornstarch)
½ tsp sweet paprika
2 medium free-range eggs
100g/3½oz (1 cup) dried
    breadcrumbs e.g. panko
2 tbsp grated Parmesan
    cheese
2 tbsp light olive oil
1 small bunch of chives,
    snipped
sea salt and freshly ground
    black pepper
green beans or broccoli,
    to serve

For the mushroom sauce:
2 tbsp light olive oil
1 small onion or 2 shallots,
    diced
1 garlic clove, crushed
300g/10oz mushrooms,
    thinly sliced
200ml/7fl oz (scant 1 cup)
    reduced fat crème fraîche

This is surprisingly filling and very easy to prepare and cook.

1 Preheat the oven to 180°C, 350°F, gas mark 4. Line a baking (cookie) sheet with foil.

2 Cut the cauliflower head, down through the stalk, into 4 thick slices. Put the cornflour and paprika in a bowl (large enough to hold a slice of cauliflower) and stir gently. Beat the eggs in another large bowl and put the breadcrumbs and Parmesan in a third.

3 Dip the cauliflower, one slice at a time, into the flour and shake off the excess before dipping into the beaten egg and, lastly, the breadcrumbs. The cauliflower slices should be well coated with crumbs.

4 Heat the oil in a large frying pan (skillet) set over a medium heat. When it's hot, fry the cauliflower slices, in batches, for 2 minutes on each side, or until starting to colour. Remove carefully and place on the foil-lined baking sheet. Bake for 15 minutes, or until golden brown and tender.

5 For the sauce, heat the oil in a pan set over a low to medium heat and cook the onion or shallots and garlic, stirring occasionally, for 5 minutes until tender. Stir in the mushrooms and cook for 5 minutes until tender and starting to colour. Reduce the heat and stir in the crème fraîche. Simmer gently for a few minutes until heated through. Season to taste with salt and pepper.

6 Serve the cauliflower schnitzels drizzled with the mushroom sauce with some green beans or broccoli on the side. Sprinkle with the chives just before serving.

OR YOU CAN TRY THIS...

– Instead of baking the cauliflower in the oven, fry it in the pan for another 6 minutes or so until tender, crisp and golden brown.

SWEET & SOUR CAULIFLOWER

SERVES: 4 | **PREP:** 20 MINUTES | **COOK:** 20 MINUTES

For the batter:
1 large free-range egg
65g/2½oz (generous ½ cup)
    cornflour (cornstarch)
a pinch of ground ginger
sea salt and black pepper

For the cauliflower and sauce:
1 medium cauliflower,
    trimmed, stem removed
    and separated into florets
1 tbsp sunflower oil
1 small onion, cut into
    chunks and separated
    into layers
1 green (bell) pepper,
    deseeded and cut into
    chunks
1 tbsp cornflour (cornstarch),
    plus extra for dusting
4 tbsp pineapple juice
2 tbsp sherry
2 tbsp rice vinegar
1 tbsp light soy sauce
juice of 1 orange
1 tbsp tomato ketchup
2 tbsp light brown sugar
100g/3½oz pineapple
    chunks (fresh or canned
    and drained)
vegetable oil, for deep-frying
boiled or steamed rice,
    to serve

Don't be put off by the long list of ingredients; this is simpler to make than it looks. You can even prepare the batter, parboil the cauliflower and make the sauce in advance. Deep-fry the cauliflower and reheat the sauce just before serving.

1 Make the batter: beat the egg and then stir in the cornflour until you have a thick, smooth mixture. Add the ginger and seasoning.

2 Cook the cauliflower florets in a pan of boiling salted water for 2 minutes. Drain in a colander and rinse under running cold water. Drain well.

3 Heat the oil in a pan or wok set over a medium to high heat and quickly stir-fry the onion and pepper until just tender.

4 Mix together the cornflour, pineapple juice, sherry, vinegar, soy sauce, orange juice, ketchup and sugar until smooth. Add to the pan and stir until thickened. If the sauce is too thick for your liking, thin it with a little water. Stir in the pineapple chunks.

5 Heat the vegetable oil in a deep pan or wok or deep-fryer, if you have one, to 190°C, 375°F (you can use a sugar thermometer to check). Meanwhile, coat the cauliflower florets with the batter and dust them with cornflour. Deep-fry them, a few at a time, for about 3 minutes until crisp and golden brown. Remove with a slotted spoon and drain on kitchen paper (paper towels).

6 Serve immediately with the sweet and sour sauce and some plain boiled or steamed rice.

OR YOU CAN TRY THIS...

– Sprinkle with sliced spring onions (scallions) for an extra crunch.
– Instead of pineapple juice use some sweet fruity jam mixed with water.
– Add some carrot matchsticks to the sauce.
– Button mushrooms can be battered and fried in the same way.

CAULIFLOWER PAD THAI

SERVES: 4 | **PREP:** 15 MINUTES | **COOK:** 10-12 MINUTES

250g/9oz flat rice noodles

1 medium cauliflower, trimmed, stem removed and separated into small florets

2 tbsp groundnut (peanut) oil

3 garlic cloves, crushed

2.5cm/1in piece fresh root ginger, peeled and diced

8 spring onions (scallions), sliced

1 red bird's eye chilli, diced

100g/3½oz (1 cup) beansprouts

50g/2oz (scant ½ cup) chopped roasted peanuts

2 tbsp sesame seeds

a handful of coriander (cilantro), chopped

lime wedges and sweet chilli sauce, to serve

For the peanut butter sauce:

5 tbsp peanut butter

3 tbsp soy sauce

1 tbsp nam pla (Thai fish sauce) or vegan fish sauce

2 tbsp palm sugar

2 tbsp tamarind paste

grated zest and juice of 2 limes

This simple dish is made with parboiled cauliflower, which is then stir-fried until golden brown, but you can also make it with spicy roasted florets. It's vegan-friendly and full of healthy goodness.

1 Place all the sauce ingredients in a bowl, add 2–3 tablespoons water and stir well to combine.

2 Prepare the rice noodles following the pack instructions. Drain.

3 Cook the cauliflower in a pan of boiling salted water for 3–4 minutes until just tender but still crisp. Drain well and pat dry with kitchen paper (paper towels).

4 Heat the oil in a wok or deep frying pan (skillet) set over a medium to high heat. Add the garlic, ginger, spring onions and chilli and stir-fry briskly for 1 minute. Add the cauliflower and cook for 2–3 minutes until golden. Stir in the peanut butter sauce, then reduce the heat and cook, covered, for 2 minutes.

5 Add the rice noodles and beansprouts and stir-fry for 1 minute, tossing them lightly.

6 Divide the mixture between 4 serving bowls. Sprinkle with the roasted peanuts, sesame seeds and coriander. Serve with lime wedges for squeezing and some sweet chilli sauce.

OR YOU CAN TRY THIS...

– Sprinkle with basil, mint or chives instead of coriander.

– Use thin rice noodles instead of thick flat ones.

– Top with some thin strips of omelette or stir in a beaten egg at the end and scramble it in the pan.

– Add some cooked prawns (shrimp) or shredded chicken.

CAULIFLOWER, CHICKEN & GORGONZOLA BAKE

SERVES: 4 | **PREP:** 10 MINUTES | **COOK:** 35-40 MINUTES

1 large cauliflower, trimmed, stem removed and separated into small florets
2 tbsp olive oil
4 skinned chicken breast fillets, sliced

For the Gorgonzola sauce:
75g/3oz (scant ½ cup) butter
50g/2oz (½ cup) plain (all-purpose) flour
600ml/1 pint (2½ cups) milk
a handful of flat-leaf parsley, chopped
200g/7oz Gorgonzola cheese, diced
sea salt and freshly ground black pepper
crusty bread or baked potatoes, to serve

Cauliflower and cheese are a combo made in heaven, and blue cheese works surprisingly well. This bake is strongly flavoured so serve it with crusty bread or plain baked potatoes.

1 Preheat the oven to 190°C, 375°F, gas mark 5.

2 Cook the cauliflower florets in a pan of boiling salted water for 3–4 minutes until just tender but still crisp. Drain well and pat dry with kitchen paper (paper towels).

3 Meanwhile, heat in the oil in a large frying pan (skillet) set over a medium to high heat and cook the chicken, turning occasionally, until cooked and golden.

4 Make the Gorgonzola sauce: melt the butter in a pan over a low heat. Add the flour and cook for 2–3 minutes, stirring with a wooden spoon, until you have a thick paste. Gradually whisk in the milk, beating until smooth. Bring to the boil, stirring all the time, until the sauce thickens. Reduce the heat to low and cook for 2–3 minutes. Off the heat, add the parsley and Gorgonzola and stir gently until the cheese melts. Season to taste.

5 Put the chicken and cauliflower in a large ovenproof dish and pour the sauce over the top. Bake for 25–30 minutes until bubbling and golden brown. Serve immediately.

OR YOU CAN TRY THIS...
– Use Dolcelatte instead of Gorgonzola.
– Use half and half broccoli and cauliflower.
– Sprinkle the finished dish with some chopped nuts.
– Toss some penne or macaroni in the sauce and top with toasted walnuts.

SIDES & PRESERVES

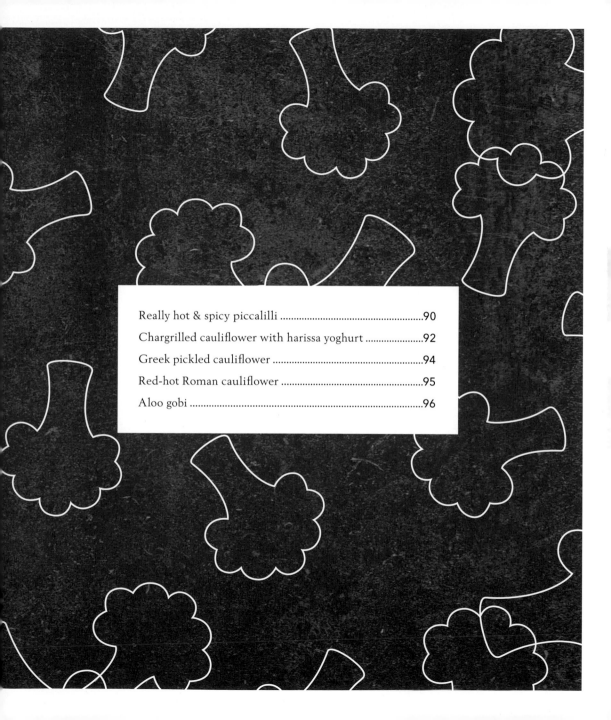

REALLY HOT & SPICY PICCALILLI

MAKES: 5-6 X 350G/12OZ JARS | **PREP:** 30 MINUTES | **SOAK:** 24 HOURS | **COOK:** 15 MINUTES

600g/1lb 6oz cauliflower florets, cut into bite-sized pieces

1.2kg/2½lb mixed vegetables, washed, trimmed and cut into bite-sized pieces

100g/3½oz (⅓ cup) salt

600ml/1 pint (2½ cups) white wine vinegar, plus 2 tbsp

200g/7oz (scant 1 cup) granulated sugar

2 tbsp English mustard powder

1 tbsp ground turmeric

1 tsp ground ginger

2 tbsp black mustard seeds

2 red or green chillies, diced

5cm/2in piece fresh root ginger, grated

2 garlic cloves, crushed

1 tbsp cornflour (cornstarch)

Cauliflower is the hero ingredient in this spicy relish but you can use a variety of other vegetables, including carrots, runner beans, courgettes (zucchini), (bell) peppers, butternut squash, pumpkin, red onions, banana shallots and cucumber. Try to resist the temptation to eat this for at least 4 weeks. The piccalilli should keep well for up to a year.

1 Put the vegetables in a large bowl and sprinkle the salt over them. Stir gently to distribute the salt evenly. Cover and set aside in a cool place for 24 hours.

2 The following day, drain off the liquid and rinse in a colander under running cold water to remove the salt. Drain and pat dry with kitchen paper (paper towels).

3 Put the vinegar, sugar, mustard, ground spices, seeds, chillies, ginger and garlic in a large pan or preserving pan and heat gently over a medium heat, stirring with a wooden spoon until the sugar dissolves. Turn up the heat and bring to the boil. Tip the vegetables into the pan and bring back to the boil, then reduce the heat to a simmer.

4 Mix the cornflour with 2 tablespoons vinegar until smooth. Add to the pan and stir gently. Simmer for 5 minutes or so until the vegetables are just tender but still retain some crunchiness and the liquid reduces and thickens.

5 Ladle the hot mixture into 5–6 hot sterilised 350g/12oz jars (see Tip), then cover with waxed discs and half-screw on the lids. Leave to cool, then tighten the lids and store in a cool dark place.

OR YOU CAN TRY THIS...

- Use brown sugar instead of white for a darker coloured pickle.
- For less heat, substitute ½–1 teaspoon crushed dried chilli flakes for the fresh chillies.
- Use traditional distilled malt vinegar instead of white wine vinegar.

TIP: To sterilise the jars, preheat the oven to 110°C, 225°F, gas mark ¼. Wash the jars in warm soapy water and dry well. Put them (lids off) in a roasting tin and place in the oven for 20–30 minutes, then turn the oven off and leave them until you're ready to fill them.

CHARGRILLED CAULIFLOWER WITH HARISSA YOGHURT

SERVES: 4 | **PREP:** 10 MINUTES | **COOK:** 8-10 MINUTES

1 medium cauliflower, trimmed, stem removed and separated into florets

olive oil, for brushing and drizzling

200g/7oz (scant 1 cup) Greek yoghurt

2 tbsp harissa

2 tbsp toasted pine nuts

1 tsp cumin seeds

sea salt and freshly ground black pepper

This makes a wonderful accompaniment to griddled chicken or some tabbouleh or couscous. Serve for an *al fresco* summer lunch when the barbecue is all fired up.

1 Cut the cauliflower florets through the stems into halves or slices and brush them with olive oil.

2 Cook over hot coals on a barbecue or in a large griddle (grill) pan set over a medium heat, turning occasionally, for about 8 minutes, or until slightly charred and tender but retaining a little 'bite'. Season to taste with salt and pepper.

3 Put the yoghurt in a bowl and swirl in the harissa.

4 Transfer the cauliflower to a serving dish and drizzle with a little olive oil. Sprinkle with the pine nuts and seeds and serve immediately, with the harissa yoghurt.

OR YOU CAN TRY THIS...

– Use your favourite hot sauce, such as Sriracha or sweet chilli.
– Add some broccoli or Romanesco florets.
– Toast the cumin seeds for more aroma and flavour.

GREEK PICKLED CAULIFLOWER

MAKES: 2 X 500G/1¼LB JARS | **PREP:** 20 MINUTES | **COOK:** 15 MINUTES

1 medium cauliflower, trimmed, stem removed and separated into florets
2 small carrots, thinly sliced
1 small courgette (zucchini), sliced
1 red (bell) pepper, deseeded and cut into bite-sized pieces
1 small fennel bulb, thinly sliced
2 large cabbage leaves
600ml/1 pint (2½ cups) white wine vinegar
1 tsp salt
120ml/4fl oz (½ cup) clear honey
3 garlic cloves, peeled
1 red chilli, deseeded and diced
1 tsp fennel seeds
1 tsp cumin seeds
1 tsp black peppercorns
1 cinnamon stick
2 bay leaves
olive oil, for sealing

In Greece, people use up a glut of summer vegetables by pickling them in vinegar with spices and herbs. Honey is sometimes used in preference to sugar. The vegetables should retain their crispness, colour and shape.

1 Add the prepared vegetables to a large pan of salted boiling water. Boil for 1 minute, then drain and refresh in iced water. Drain well and divide between 2 hot sterilised 500g/1¼lb jars (see Tip on page 91) with a cabbage leaf on top to stop the vegetables from rising to the top in the next step.

2 Pour 300ml/½ pint (1¼ cups) water into a pan and add the vinegar, salt, honey, garlic, chilli, seeds, spices and bay leaves. Boil for 5 minutes, then reduce the heat and simmer for 5 minutes.

3 Pour the hot pickling liquid over the vegetables in the jars and add some olive oil to each jar to seal it. Screw on the lids, or if you're using Mason jars, cover with the glass tops.

4 Store in a cool dark place for at least 1 week before using. After opening, keep in the fridge.

OR YOU CAN TRY THIS...
– Use any seasonal herbs and vegetables – try green beans, celery, cabbage, broccoli, etc.
– Add an onion, quartered and separated into layers.

RED-HOT ROMAN CAULIFLOWER

SERVES: 4 | **PREP:** 5 MINUTES | **COOK:** 15 MINUTES

1 large cauliflower
3 tbsp fruity green olive oil
2 dried red chillies, diced
3 garlic cloves, crushed
1 sprig of rosemary, leaves
    stripped
sea salt crystals

You will often find this simple dish in Roman trattorie, made with cauliflower, its green Romanesco cousin or even broccoli. Serve it as a side dish or tossed with pasta shapes (penne works well) and dredged with grated Parmesan. It even works well as a topping for toasted ciabatta or sourdough bread.

1 Trim the cauliflower stalk and cut it into slices. Discard any leaves and remove all the florets.

2 Cook the sliced stalk and florets in a large pan of salted boiling water for about 5 minutes, or until the florets are just tender but not mushy. Drain well.

3 Heat the olive oil in a large frying pan (skillet) set over a low heat. Add the chillies and their seeds and cook very gently for 5 minutes to release their aroma and colour. Add the garlic and rosemary leaves and cook for 1 minute.

4 Increase the heat to medium and add the cauliflower. Cook for 4–5 minutes, turning it occasionally. Season to taste with sea salt.

5 Serve hot as an accompaniment to griddled meat or sautéed chicken escalopes.

OR YOU CAN TRY THIS...
– Add some diced anchovies with the garlic.
– Add some crispy bacon lardons or cubed pancetta.
– Cook some diced red (bell) pepper with the chillies and garlic.
– Use fresh red chillies instead of dried ones.

ALOO GOBI

SERVES: 4 | **PREP:** 20 MINUTES | **COOK:** 35-40 MINUTES

4 tbsp sunflower or
 rapeseed oil
1 tsp cumin seeds
1 tbsp black mustard seeds
400g/14oz potatoes, peeled
 and cubed
1 medium cauliflower,
 trimmed, stem removed
 and separated into florets
1 red onion, thinly sliced
4 garlic cloves, crushed
2.5cm/1in piece fresh root
 ginger, peeled and diced
350g/12oz tomatoes,
 roughly chopped
2 tsp ground coriander
1 tsp chilli powder
½ tsp ground turmeric
2 long red chillies, halved
 lengthways
juice of 1 lime
a handful of coriander
 (cilantro), chopped
sea salt
boiled rice, warm chapatis
 or naan bread, to serve

This classic dish of spicy cauliflower with potatoes is cooked in homes all over India. The spices vary from region to region but the basics stay the same. Serve it with some boiled rice, warm chapatis or naan bread.

1 Heat the oil in a wide pan set over a medium heat. Cook the seeds for 1–2 minutes until they start to pop and release their aroma.

2 Add the potatoes and cook for 6–8 minutes, stirring occasionally, or until golden brown all over. Remove and drain on kitchen paper (paper towels).

3 Add the cauliflower to the pan and cook, stirring from time to time, for 5–6 minutes, or until golden brown. Remove and drain on kitchen paper.

4 Add the onion to the pan and cook, stirring occasionally, for 6–8 minutes until tender. Add the garlic and ginger and cook for 1 minute, then stir in the tomatoes, spices and chillies. Cook for 4–5 minutes until the tomatoes soften.

5 Return the potatoes and cauliflower to the pan together with a little water to moisten everything. Reduce the heat to low, cover the pan and simmer gently for 10 minutes or so until all the vegetables are tender and the liquid has reduced. Check to make sure it's not too dry – if so, just add some more water and cook a little longer.

6 Season to taste with sea salt and stir in the lime juice. Serve sprinkled with coriander.

OR YOU CAN TRY THIS...
– Add some fresh or frozen peas or shredded spinach.
– Stir in a teaspoon of garam masala at the end.
– Serve with raita or Indian pickles.

BAKING

CAULIFLOWER CHOCOLATE BROWNIES

MAKES: 16 | **PREP:** 20 MINUTES | **COOK:** 35-40 MINUTES

100g/3½oz (½ cup) butter, plus extra for greasing
1 small cauliflower, trimmed, stem removed and separated into florets
225g/8oz dark (semisweet) chocolate, broken into pieces
3 medium free-range eggs
225g/8oz (1 cup) brown sugar
175g/6oz (generous 1 cup) ground almonds (almond meal)
4 tbsp cocoa (unsweetened chocolate) powder
1 tsp baking powder
a few drops of vanilla extract
50g/2oz (½ cup) chopped walnuts
icing (confectioner's) sugar, for dusting

Crisp on the outside, squidgy on the inside and oozing with chocolate, nobody will ever believe that the secret ingredient that adds moistness to these delicious brownies is cauliflower. And what's more, they are gluten-free.

1 Preheat the oven to 190°C, 375°F, gas mark 5. Grease a 20cm/8in square baking tin (pan) with butter and line with baking parchment.

2 Steam the cauliflower over a pan of simmering water for 10 minutes, or until softened. Leave to cool and then purée in a food processor.

3 Meanwhile, melt the chocolate and butter in a heatproof bowl over a pan of gently simmering water.

4 Add the melted chocolate and butter and eggs to the food processor and blitz with the cauliflower. Add the sugar, ground almonds, cocoa powder, baking powder and vanilla and blitz again until smooth. Fold in the walnuts, distributing them evenly throughout the mixture.

5 Spoon the mixture into the prepared baking tin, pushing it into the corners, and level the top. Bake for 25–30 minutes, or until risen and crusty on top and round the edges. Insert a thin metal skewer into the centre – if it comes out clean, the brownies are cooked.

6 Leave to cool in the tin before dusting the top with icing sugar. Cut into squares and serve. The brownies will keep well for up to 5 days in an airtight container.

OR YOU CAN TRY THIS...
– Use chopped hazelnuts or pecans instead of walnuts.
– Add some grated orange zest, a pinch of chilli powder or crushed dried chilli flakes.

CHEESY CAULIFLOWER BREAKFAST MUFFINS

SERVES: 12 | **PREP:** 15 MINUTES | **COOK:** 25-30 MINUTES

1 small cauliflower, trimmed, stem removed and separated into small florets
2 medium free-range eggs
250ml/8fl oz (1 cup) buttermilk
120ml/4fl oz (½ cup) olive oil
225g/8oz (2¼ cups) self-raising (self-rising) flour
½ tsp baking powder
2 tsp wholegrain mustard
50g/2oz (½ cup) grated Parmesan cheese
50g/2oz (½ cup) grated Cheddar cheese, plus extra for sprinkling
4 spring onions (scallions), diced
1 bunch of chives, snipped
sea salt and freshly ground black pepper

A savoury muffin and a vegetable juice or fruit smoothie makes a really quick and healthy breakfast. These muffins are good to eat on-the-go or to take to work as a delicious packed lunch.

1 Preheat the oven to 200°C, 400°F, gas mark 6. Line a 12-hole muffin tin with paper muffin cases.

2 Put the cauliflower florets in a food processor and blitz into tiny pieces, as small as possible.

3 Beat the eggs, buttermilk and olive oil until well combined, then season with salt and pepper. Sift the flour and baking powder into a bowl and make a well in the centre. Pour in the beaten egg mixture and stir gently. Stir in the cauliflower, mustard, grated cheeses, spring onions and chives. Be careful not to over-mix. Don't worry about the odd small lump.

4 Divide the mixture between the paper cases and sprinkle with a little grated Cheddar. Bake for 25–30 minutes until risen and golden brown. Test whether the muffins are cooked by inserting a thin skewer into the centre – it should come out clean. Cool on a wire rack.

5 These muffins are best eaten warm or at room temperature. They will keep well for 2–3 days in an airtight container.

OR YOU CAN TRY THIS...
– Add some diced cooked bacon or ham.
– Add some chopped chilli or crushed dried chilli flakes.
– Add some crushed garlic or garlic powder.
– Sprinkle with panko breadcrumbs before cooking.

CAULIFLOWER PEANUT BUTTER COOKIES

MAKES: APPROXIMATELY 15 | **PREP:** 15 MINUTES | **COOK:** 10 MINUTES

250g/9oz (1 cup) smooth peanut butter

120ml/4fl oz (½ cup) maple syrup

150g/5oz (1 cup) ground almonds (almond meal)

115g/4oz (1 cup) cauliflower rice (see page 11)

1 tsp bicarbonate of soda (baking soda)

a pinch of grated nutmeg

a good pinch of ground cinnamon

50g/2oz (scant ½ cup) chopped peanuts

These gluten-free and vegan-friendly cookies are so easy to make, and the chopped peanuts give them a lovely crunchy texture.

1 Preheat the oven to 180°C, 350°F, gas mark 4. Line 2 baking (cookie) sheets with baking parchment.

2 Mix together the peanut butter and maple syrup in a bowl. Stir in the ground almonds, cauliflower rice, nutmeg, cinnamon and bicarbonate of soda until well combined. Stir in the peanuts, distributing them evenly throughout the mixture.

3 Drop rounded tablespoons of the mixture on to the lined baking sheets, leaving some space in between, and flatten them a little by pressing down gently with a fork.

4 Bake for about 10 minutes until golden brown and firm to the touch.

5 Leave to cool before eating. Store the cookies in an airtight container for up to 7 days.

OR YOU CAN TRY THIS...
– Add a few drops of vanilla extract.
– Use crunchy peanut butter instead of smooth.

CAULIFLOWER CHOCOLATE CHIP COOKIES

MAKES: APPROXIMATELY 20 | **PREP:** 15 MINUTES | **COOK:** 10 MINUTES

115g/4oz (1 cup) cauliflower rice (see page 11)

115g/4oz (generous ½ cup) butter, diced

175g/6oz (¾ cup) soft brown sugar

1 tsp vanilla extract

1 medium free-range egg

175g/6oz (1½ cups) plain (all-purpose) flour

¼ tsp salt

1 tsp bicarbonate of soda (baking soda)

175g/6oz (1 cup) dark (semisweet) chocolate chips

These crisp cookies are slightly chewy in the centre and will leave you wanting more. The cauliflower adds moistness and depth of flavour to the mix.

1 Preheat the oven to 180°C, 350°F, gas mark 4. Line 2 baking (cookie) sheets with baking parchment.

2 Put the cauliflower rice in a heatproof glass bowl, cover with clingfilm (plastic wrap) and microwave on high for 3–4 minutes. Spoon the cauliflower on to a stack of kitchen paper (paper towels) or a clean tea towel and press out any liquid until the grains are dry.

3 Beat the butter and sugar until light and fluffy (you can do this in a food mixer or with an electric whisk). Beat in the vanilla and the egg, then stir in the cauliflower rice. Sift in the flour, salt and bicarbonate of soda and fold into the mixture with the chocolate chips, distributing them evenly throughout.

4 Drop rounded tablespoons of the mixture on to the lined baking sheets, leaving some space in between, and flatten them a little. Bake for about 10 minutes until golden brown and firm to the touch.

5 Leave to cool before eating. Store the cookies in an airtight container for up to 7 days.

OR YOU CAN TRY THIS...
– Add some chopped pecans or walnuts.
– Add a pinch of ground cinnamon.

CHEESY CAULIFLOWER APERITIF CAKE

SERVES: 6 | **PREP:** 25 MINUTES | **COOK:** 1 HOUR

1 medium cauliflower,
   trimmed, stem removed
   and separated into florets
5 tbsp olive oil
1 red onion, finely chopped
1 red chilli, deseeded and
   diced
1 tbsp chopped rosemary
   leaves
1 tbsp chopped thyme
   leaves
200g/7oz baby spinach
6 medium free-range eggs
115g/4oz (generous 1 cup)
   self-raising (self-rising)
   flour
1 tsp baking powder
1 tsp smoked paprika
½ tsp sea salt
100g/3½oz soft goat's
   cheese
50g/2oz diced feta cheese

Serve this savoury cake cut into thin slices with an aperitif – a Campari soda or Aperol spritz is good – before an *al fresco* dinner with friends. It's also great for picnics.

1 Preheat the oven to 200°C, 400°F, gas mark 6. Line a 23cm/9in loose base (springform) cake tin (pan) with baking parchment.

2 Cook the cauliflower florets in a pan of boiling salted water for 15 minutes, or until the florets are really soft but retain their shape. Drain well and pat dry with kitchen paper (paper towels).

3 Meanwhile, heat the oil in a large pan set over a low to medium heat and cook the red onion, chilli and chopped herbs, stirring occasionally, for 8–10 minutes until softened. Stir in the spinach and cook, covered, for 2 minutes until it wilts. Remove from the heat and leave to cool.

4 Tip the cooled onion and spinach mixture into a large bowl or a food mixer. Add the eggs and beat well. Sift in the flour, baking powder, smoked paprika and salt and beat until well combined. Gently stir in the cheeses and the cauliflower florets.

5 Pour the mixture into the prepared tin and level the top. Bake for 40–45 minutes until risen and golden brown. Test whether the cake is cooked by inserting a thin skewer into the centre – it should come out clean. Leave to cool in the tin before turning out.

6 Serve, cut into slices, at room temperature. Store in an airtight container for up to 3 days.

OR YOU CAN TRY THIS...
– Use gram (chickpea) flour plus an extra spoonful of baking powder.
– Grated Parmesan, Grana Padano or Cheddar can be substituted for goat's cheese.
– Add chopped basil or dill.
– Add some ground turmeric or cumin seeds.

1

Published in 2021 by Ebury Press an imprint of Ebury Publishing,
20 Vauxhall Bridge Road,
London SW1V 2SA

Ebury Press is part of the Penguin Random House group of companies
whose addresses can be found at global.penguinrandomhouse.com

Penguin
Random House
UK

Text copyright © Ebury Press 2021
Design copyright © Ebury Press 2021
Photography copyright © Ebury Press 2021

Heather Thomas has asserted her right to be identified as the author of this
Work in accordance with the Copyright, Designs and Patents Act 1988

Design: Louise Evans
Photography: Joff Lee
Food stylist: Mari Williams
Editor: Sam Crisp

First published by Ebury Press in 2021

www.penguin.co.uk

A CIP catalogue record for this book is available from the British Library

ISBN 9781529106039

Printed and bound in China by Toppan Leefung